The Garden of Love

Our Inner Wealth

The Garden of Love

Our Inner Wealth

Manuela Timofte

Editing and cover: Manuela Timofte

Image cover: Pexels.com

Published by Manuela Timofte

Copyright © 2024 de Manuela Timofte

Published in Romania

To my son,

Alex

Content

Content   7

Foreword   11

Introduction   15

1. Knowledge of the Mind and Wisdom of the Soul   19

    Knowledge - good or bad?   24

    AYNI Principle   27

    Energy and vibration   34

    O moment of LOVE   46

2. Mind and Obstacles   51

    The Garden of "selfishness"   65

    Fear   67

    Selfishness   75

    Failure   89

3. Army of Fears   91

    Procrastination   93

    Repression   97

    Confirmation   100

    Comparison   101

    Standardization   105

    Hypocrisy   108

    False Assumption   113

    Disappointment   114

    Mockery   117

    Cowardice   118

    Indifference   119

    False Security   124

    Resignation   126

    Fake responsibility   128

    Despair   129

    Victimization   131

4. Thoughts, Words and Deeds   135

    With and without mask   140

    A Society without masks   143

    Free Thinking   144

5. Soul Flowers   149

    Forgiveness   152

    Respect   159

    Truth   164

    Sincerity   171

    Faith   174

Courage   186
Responsibility   187
6. Soul Wealth   **193**
Love lessons   197
Love   202
Gratitude   213
7. Love Garden   **217**
Our Inner Wealth   219
References   **227**
About the Author   **229**

"When we achieve full understanding and knowledge, we will comprehend the great mystery of our ancestors."

Pavel Coruț (34)

Foreword

The words in this book originated from the aspirations of a ten-year-old girl to make the world a better place for everyone, especially for future generations.

She often came home from school crying because she didn't understand why so many people she had come to know in this world let her down, and she knew deep down that all people were good. She was too young at that age to understand that the goodness she knew existed in everyone really does exist; it's just hidden beneath the emotions, traumas, and experiences of everyone's past. What she had lived up to that age had already imprinted on her subconsciously the lack of value and the need to look for it externally, so she had started on the path of conquering a false value that would give her perfection. She had no way of knowing that she was living an illusion that only existed in the false norms of a selfish society.

Being that crying little girl, I longed and searched for years for the answers that would give me that perfection, only that all I found were the solutions offered by reason, following the patterns recorded in me by the ancestral heritage, to which I added my own experiences. Nothing seemed permanent, and thus, I was only experiencing temporary illusions.

Now, in the inner peace I have discovered, I am grateful every morning when I open my eyes and can get out of bed to embrace whatever life has in store for me. The difference is that now I'm not searching or expecting; I'm simply living each day as it comes. I acknowledge that my experiences have been shaped by my thoughts, emotions, and actions. I have learned to express gratitude for all the good and bad in my life, and particularly for the opportunity to continue learning the lessons I am meant to learn during my time on earth.

Since everything I write comes from my own feelings and experiences, and the lessons that life has taught me, the words I express are not intended to seek anyone's approval, nor do I aim to persuade anyone. My experiences have shaped me, and while I cannot change others, they have certainly changed me. I share these words with you, the reader, as a fellow human being, with a life full of both pains and joys, fears and anxiety. By seeking and taking action towards the change I believed in, I have transformed my life.

This transformation doesn't mean that I have gained material riches or external value. What I have attained from my internal struggles is personal growth and the rediscovery of the inner wealth that exists in each of us. I have found contentment in each day I live and the inner peace I have been seeking for so long. I have realized that the key to unlocking the door to spiritual freedom is within each of us. It took me decades to uncover the truth that it was hidden within my soul, so close, yet elusive.

*Why did I call this book "Garden of Love"? On the one hand, it's my joy and gratitude for what the earth offers us, especially in the form of the colour, tenderness, and indescribable beauty of flowers. On the other hand, it's my belief that all that is good and beautiful in every human being **is a garden of love.***

In our real garden, we may prefer certain flowers and try to "eradicate" certain weeds, but the flowers and weeds inside us define us as people and the life we lead. Just as in the real garden, we have the choice whether to protect or leave ourselves prey to the weeds that grow at will, even leaving the entire garden in ruins. Giving our care and love to the garden is similar to what we give from within to those around us. Whether we offer flowers of love or weeds of hatred and malice, we receive the same from others. Everything we send out into the Universe comes back to us tenfold. The decision of what we grow, care for, and offer or not is ours.

From the love I have always had for flowers, because they have always been by my side regardless of life's events, I offer these lines to the flowers in the garden of our soul - forgiveness, respect, courage, truth - with love and gratitude.

I hope that by choosing to read this book, you can find the flowers you like, and the lines that will resonate with you; and that they give you colour, fragrance, understanding, and lots of love.

Manuela

❀⁛ᧁᧁ⁛❀

Introduction
We only reap what we sow

The beauty, colour, and tenderness of flowers accompany us throughout our lives. They are silent witnesses to our experiences, enhancing our joy, comforting sadness, easing suffering, and offering hope. They are present from the moment we are born until we die. We are baptized with flowers, married among flowers, and covered with them in death. Personally, I agree with Okakura Kakuzo that "the very idea of conceiving a world without flowers is terrifying" (29).

Although flowers have a short 'life' they bravely face all weathers, accepting heat and cold, rain and storms with equal grace. We, like flowers, enjoy the cooling rain on hot summer days but dislike it when it brings storms and havoc. We revel in the warmth of the sun, yet when the heat persists, we long for rain and coolness. Excess of any kind disrupts the balance of life.

Life proves this to us in full, therefore, it is not just a straight and easy road. It has ups and downs, and we go up to go down. Even if we don't like it, we fall to learn to get up and move forward. We are not made to live in monotony. We may think that just as driving for a long time on a straight road without any bumps or curves bores us and makes us sleepy, so we need life changes. We need salt and pepper, a mix of good and bad experiences to find the balance we lost somewhere, sometimes.

I have learned from the story "Salt in Dishes," which I read many times as a child, that life is not limited to what gives us sweetness or makes us happy. Life includes the salt of its lessons because, taken together, sugar and salt give flavour. While salt and sugar may look the same, they taste different. They are not good when used alone, but they are flavourful when used to enhance other things.

Both are important in our lives, yet each can harm us if in too much or too little quantity. As Harald W. Tietze says, any excess makes a thing medicine or poison (13).

We all desire a beautiful life, by that, we mean to have no part of bad, of salt and pepper. However, life includes them all to complete the picture of harmony, as love isn't just about sweetness and happiness. We live both good and bad because the Universe ensures that everything keeps its balance. Confucian thinking says that, the optimal path is harmony, in all things, while Schopenhauer says "Every man needs worries, misery, pain, just as a ship needs ballast to float alone and straight to the target". (5)

On my journey to rediscover myself and find balance in life, I have always found solace in the presence of flowers. They have been there for both my moments of joy and sadness, through smiles and tears. I have always loved them, planting them wherever I find a place that could use some beauty.

They also accompanied my selfishness in the houses I lived in, being present in pots. My change made me want to let them become part of the nature I enjoy every day, in the garden, or free in the field, not constrained by conditions that my mind decided to confine them in pots, between four walls, a right that I as a human have arrogated to myself to change their destiny and turn them into my personal companion.

Gratitude for these small miracles of the planet exists from the moment I look at the seed I lovingly plant in the ground. I am happy and grateful for each of the flowers as they bloom, slowly, and then, as time passes, my joy is enveloped in their colour, fragrance and tenderness. Each flower is a miracle born from a smaller or larger seed, but each one is true to its nature. They each have their own unique beauty and they do not compete with each other. They live their lives for as long as they last, but unconditionally offer their colour, tenderness, and fragrance to all who wish to appreciate them.

I want to thank them for being in my life, so I take care of them. I take responsibility for what I plant, offering them my trust that they will become what I want them to be. I respect them for who they are and feel gratitude for all they give me. I also forgive them if they are not what my selfishness wants them to be. I am thankful for their existence and I give them love.

I also like to think of our life as a corner of nature or a garden. All that is beautiful and good in every person brings happiness to them and to others. The things that are harmful to ourselves and others are like weeds that we need to acknowledge and thank for showing us that the flowers dear to us can wither and die if they are not cared for.

The examples you will find in the book, scattered among the weeds or flowers, are pieces of the puzzle of my life, which have helped to define me as the person I am now. They are part of the path followed by me, a path of rediscovering the spiritual wealth through which I understood how rich we all are and as Schopenhauer (5) calls it, a condition of happiness.

Just as the flowers in the garden need our presence to protect them from unwanted weeds, so we need to deal with the weeds that grow and invade our souls. It is not an easy path, but I know that in order to live life the way I want, I have learned two important things: **nothing is impossible, and where the desire comes from the heart, there is always a way to reach it.**

The decision to nurture those flowers of the soul is a personal choice and it is not so important how much others love you, but rather how much love and kindness you give to others from the flowers of your soul garden. As writer Alexandru Vlahuță says,

Manuela Timofte

"Whether or not you, the traveler of the fleeting moment, enjoy the fruits of the tree you plant is of little consequence. What truly matters is that the tree you plant bears fruit." (44)

"Whether or not you, the traveler of the fleeting moment, enjoy the fruits of the tree you plant is of little consequence. What truly matters is that the tree you plant bears fruit." (44)

1. Knowledge of the Mind and Wisdom of the Soul

Knowledge is limited. Imagination envelops the world.
Albert Einstein (44)

We often hear Francis Bacon's expression, "Knowledge is power" (44). What knowledge are we talking about? What knowledge do we apply in our daily lives?

I flashback over ten years ago, on a summer morning, when the sun slowly begins its familiar journey across the sky.

I'm running down the edge of town, something I do every morning. At this time of the morning, few people are on the road. I only met one owner who took his dog/dogs for a walk. I cross to the other side of the road and see myself running further, looking fondly at everything that comes my way as if my path intersects with the lives of others. I pass houses, the school, and the sports field until I reach the outskirts of the city. There, my imagination runs wild as I enjoy the lush green grass, and the freely growing flowers all warmed by the sun's rays. It is a place where the trees stand like ancient giants forgotten by time, living their peaceful existence. I look at them and express my gratitude for their existence, admiring their branches with their leaves glistening in the sunlight and... It makes me smile—it's all so beautiful, fascinating and interesting!

Each tree has an abundance of leaves, and upon closer inspection, no two are identical, even if they belong to the same tree and branch. They come in different sizes and brightness, and they neither appear nor die all at once. Despite their differences, they share the same tree and branch, and they do not harm each other. Throughout their brief life of a few seasons, they all coexist and their sole purpose is to help the tree grow from one year to the next.

The tree appears to me as the most beautiful example of life that nature offers to humanity. We are all humans, entering the world in the same way. Despite this, we are incredibly diverse, not only physically but also in terms of our thoughts, emotions, and experiences. Similar to the leaves on trees, we are just temporary visitors on this planet; we do not all arrive and depart simultaneously. We are born on different branches of nations and cultures. However, unlike the leaves, we struggle to make room for each other.

We exist within a universe whose origins and ultimate fate are unknown. It is a universe where nothing is arbitrary and everything follows a system that mankind is still striving to comprehend, a system that operates according to its own laws. Beyond all this, we feel powerful when we possess knowledge. But what kind of knowledge are we referring to? Is it a knowledge of the mind, a wisdom of the soul, or a combination of both?

Some of us read, learn, and acquire degrees, yet we still understand so little. On the other hand, there are those individuals, (I do not know about you, but I have encountered in my life), whom we refer to as "ordinary people." They may not have received formal education or have only had limited schooling, but they amaze us with their extensive knowledge and understanding of life, often without having read books, especially scientific or motivational ones. They have solutions to problems that some of us struggle with for a long time, ultimately giving up or seeking answers from others with higher levels of education than us. These ordinary individuals learn from life's lessons, glean wisdom from nature, remember their mistakes, and humbly and respectfully pass on their teachings to those who are willing to listen.

At the same time, children have the remarkable ability to express profound insights about life despite their young age, that prove a high understanding of life, without having gone through it. They demonstrate a wisdom we usually attribute to those who have reached the age of senescence. We watch them or listen to them in awe because they only call things by their names, which we, adults with education and years of life experience, do not have the courage or *with all our rational thinking, did not see things the way they present it. Children say what they feel without restriction, until we, the educated, start building barriers of their minds. We are the ones who seek a knowledge and a so-called morality, while we think too much only in the patterns we grew up in and which were imposed on us by those who know how to control the masses of people.*

Furthermore, nature provides us with invaluable lessons through its continuous connection with the universe. Despite lacking formal education, nature's resilience and ability to endure various challenges: the heat, the storms, the snow, the "death" to which we, those who call ourselves civilized beings, offer it. Every living organism follows the inherent wisdom of its seed, demonstrating the natural order of growth and development. Oaks will not grow from flower seeds, just as tomatoes will not grow from oak acorns. It seems normal to us even without learning in botany classes.

The sun rises and sets every day, and no one knows since or until when. Trees change their attire with the seasons, according to their own understanding. Flowers grow and bloom following the knowledge stored in the tiny seed from which they are born. Nature always reminds us that she will endure no matter how much we destroy it because it knows to regenerate coming back to life again.

Water holds information, researchers tell us. Dr. Masaru Emoto (22) impregnated water crystals with different energies corresponding to certain words and showed us that water molecules react to thoughts and feelings. But can we, who are 70% water like our planet, understand the negative or beneficial influence our thoughts and words have on our body and the planet?

We simply know and accept many things about nature, drawing from our inner knowing, without asking why it is not otherwise. However, when it comes to human nature, we tend to ask numerous questions and seek answers externally, often disregarding the knowledge that comes from within. This internal knowledge seems to have been neglected in favour of seeking external light. As a result, we remain unaware of many aspects of ourselves, leaving ourselves trapped in the matrices of society, in the chains of fears that we have and which, the few, who know what power lies in each man, know how to manipulate so that soul knowledge is not believed. Thus, they know and manipulate those fears to prevent the power of man, and this knowledge from emerging.

Individuals who follow the wisdom of their soul are often labeled as "chosen" or successful. They are the ones who carve their own paths, pursuing their dreams and desires rather than conforming to societal expectations. Unlike many who prioritize comfort and abandon their aspirations due to fatigue or fear, successful individuals do not give up on their goals. They are guided by the wisdom of their soul and use their reasoning. They are unafraid of failure, viewing it as a valuable learning experience. Similarly, they do not fear obstacles, recognizing that each one serves a purpose in their lives, providing necessary lessons and knowledge. Moreover, they seize every opportunity that comes their way, determined to achieve their goals. These individuals listen to their intuition, that cosmic library encoded within our DNA (33) and complement it with knowledge from their minds.

Knowledge - good or bad?

We often label knowledge as either good or bad, but isn't its value determined by how it is used? Isn't how the access to knowledge was given and the limits imposed part of the basis of the ignorance and darkness in which the many struggle? A darkness where some only dream and others really seek enlightenment?

According to Lao Tze, humanity gradually lost knowledge, virtue, kindness, and justice, instead favouring empty ceremonies as a substitute for true virtue. This led to chaos, as "False knowledge is the appearance of the Path and the beginning of stupidity" (18).

The appearance of the path is obscured by the misuse of all that humanity has discovered, which is often not used for the benefit of humanity. Whether it's natural resources freely given by the Mother Earth or ancient knowledge kept hidden and exclusive by a few, everything has been turned into a tool to instil fear in the minds of many and a source to create wealth, a material power but a false one for the soul. Consequently, what was once known to humanity became forbidden, plunging humanity into chaos, pain, and darkness.

The knowledge that most of us live with is the one that our rational thinking creates, dividing the world into "I" and everything else. However, this separation is a falsehood created by our minds, fuelled by ignorance. I use the term ignorance because many of us are not aware of the unity of the Universe, a concept Eastern philosophies have spoken about and modern physics also considers. Fred Hoyle mentioned by Fritoj Kapra in Theophysics (12), says that if a part were missing from the Universe, our existence would not be the same, because what we live daily is so connected to the macroscopic aspects of the Universe that it is impossible for them not be seen as a unit.

As humans, we often see ourselves as separate from the earth, despite being temporary tenants on this planet. It is within our power to decide how we use the resources provided by Earth. Our ancestors revered and cherished nature as they lived in harmony with it. Even today, we can observe harmony in villages where individuals work the land with love and care for nature. Romania's villages are a perfect example of this, with the Prince of Wales expressing his admiration for the harmony between the local population and nature, which attracted him to Transylvania.

If we are honest with ourselves, deep down we all desire to live in harmony with our environment. However, our way of living has become excessively self-centred, often neglecting the impact we have on our surroundings. Do the majority of us truly live in harmony with Mother Earth?

We often regard ourselves as owners of the planet, even though we are merely temporary inhabitants. Over generations, our stay has led to an exploitation of Earth - constructing, demolishing, deforesting, and haphazardly discarding our waste. We have caused harm to Mother Earth. What legacy are we leaving for future generations? What knowledge guides our actions? What knowledge is bequeathed to future generations when we act selfishly and greedily? With this acting, we fail to pass down knowledge to the coming generations. These actions demonstrate our lack of harmony with nature, reflecting our own inner disharmony. To be in harmony with nature means being in harmony with everyone's nature, as per the TAO teaching (12).

We are essentially tenants on this land, and everything is borrowed for the duration of our lives. In truth, we inherit nothing from the earth; we only borrow it from our descendants. We own nothing except for our thoughts and feelings. We enter this world with nothing material, and we depart in the same manner. Yet, our minds make us see life through the lens of the things and people we gather around us. However, life is all that surrounds us. It is every tree and every flower. "Plants have life, minds and "souls", as well as have the animals, man and super-man." says the Kybalion (39).

Life revolves around accumulation and giving, receiving and giving back. Chinese wisdom dictates that everything contains both an entrance and an exit, a Yin and a Yang - that's the way it is.

The planet itself is a living being and supplies us with everything we need for survival. Its life is an expression of kindness, love, and altruism as it respects the AYNI principle...

What are we contributing in return?

AYNI Principle

The AYNI Principle emphasizes equality, respect, and mutual giving and receiving, because we all are interconnected. According to this principle, our actions, whether good or bad, will come back to us in some form or another. The more we give, the more we will receive, and the only way to receive is to give.

Our upbringing and education often lead us to expect the consequences of our actions to come directly from the people to whom we have given. However, in reality, these consequences may come from elsewhere, at the right place and time. When we are wronged by someone, it's important to consider that we too may have wronged others. We may not want to admit our own selfishness, but our minds are often seeking reasons to give with the expectation of receiving something in return – whether it's a service that can help us advance socially or a financial gain.

Despite our expectations, the laws of the universe are impartial and operate uniformly for everyone. The person who has treated us well or wronged us is simply an instrument of the universe, facilitating our recompense or repayment for our actions toward others. This understanding allows us to reflect how much harm we have caused each other and the earth. By acknowledging that our actions stem from selfishness, we can better understand and no longer be surprised by all the disasters we experience.

In the Inca tradition, the fundamental law of life is AYNI, which means sacred reciprocity. Without this reciprocity, there is disharmony, chaos, and suffering. Therefore, we need to practice reciprocity to restore harmony.

From a selfish perspective, we tend to live without recognizing our interconnectedness to everything in the universe, and man is connected to living nature through neurons and his abilities: telepathy, and psychokinesis. Being preoccupied with our fears, worries, hopes and interests and their satisfaction, we ignore that we are connected to everything that exists, says Carlos Castaneda (6). As a result, we tend to exploit the earth without expressing true gratitude or reciprocity, both to the Earth and to each other as humans. We take without giving and gather without wanting to give because we perceive giving as a loss. However, love comes with gratitude. This is the essence of sacred reciprocity and the Incas consider it the main principle of life. According to Andean thought, living in harmony with creation means that creation will also live in harmony with us. (23)

Man is emotion, energy in motion, and there is an energy matrix in every living being (21) that has a shape similar to the body, according to Dan Farcaș (8). Trees, rivers, birds, animals, computers, cars, clouds, and rain - everything is energy, as understood by shamanic tribes and confirmed by science. Each of us generates a magnetic field that varies in strength. Being connected to the source from which we come, our positive or negative thoughts, emotions and actions leave their mark on our world.

Whatever we do has consequences. We are caught in a circle where any action of ours begets another action. Every event has a cause, and our thoughts and actions have their effects in what the

Kybalion (39) calls the great chain of causes. In AYNI it is sacred reciprocity, in Buddhism the chain of cause and effect is samsara, and karma is its engine. In scientific language, the immense cosmic mechanism is perfectly determined because it obeys the law of cause and effect. (12)

Therefore, everything in life becomes a cause that will have effects, and everything that becomes excess will bring imbalances in life and in our world. By acting out of selfishness, we will attract events that deprive us of beautiful emotions and fill us with panic, anxiety, repression, and false assumptions. Should we lament our impoverished or painful lives when we are the architects of it, when we are the ones who create it for ourselves? What answer can we give to Pavel Coruţ's questions: "Do you know what would happen if one day the trees decided to respond to people with the same measure? Do you know what fantastic power lies hidden in trees and plants? Have you thought what would happen if minerals stopped obeying humans?" (34)

By treating those around us and the earth with respect, we honor the AYNI principle, which emphasizes the interconnectedness of all living beings. Nature abides by this principle, as it gives back what civilization, driven by the knowledge of the mind, has taken away. The planet follows this principle, but do we as humans?

The Ayni principle can be understood as the universal law of cause and effect, which was recognized by ancient Egyptian sages and is expressed as one of the hermetic principles of truth in the Kybalion. This principle, known as the Principle of Cause and Effect, states that "Every cause has its effect; every effect has its cause; everything happens according to the law. Hazard is a name for an unknown law. There are many levels of causality, but nothing escapes the law" (39).

Yet, despite these universal laws, we humans have established our own laws that, born of selfishness, prioritize reason and the concept of taking and receiving.

Throughout history, those who defied these laws by choosing intuition and knowledge derived from their own reasoning were severely punished or even lost their lives. Knowledge was forbidden, and the power of the church and the inquisition was invoked to torture or burn "witches and sinners" at the stake under the pretext that "knowledge is of the devil".

Thus, the human mind was only directed in a certain direction by those who came into possession of the knowledge which is normally the right of every soul that comes to this earth. Today, even though we consider ourselves civilized, many important pieces of knowledge have been forbidden. Entire libraries have been burned, documents hidden, and archaeological discoveries destroyed. As a result, the human mind has been limited by those who control the knowledge that rightfully belongs to every individual. Those who try to share by writing, filming, discussing hidden knowledge or expressing different opinions are often silenced, exiled, harmed or injured. Books and films that offer alternative perspectives are sometimes banned or suppressed. Many who are not killed are sidelined, and isolated, and negative propaganda is made against them. Many people are afraid to consider other viewpoints due to the fear tactics used by those in control. Often, we rely solely on information provided by social media, which limits our access to different ideas. This lack of knowledge and the comfort of the familiar leads to the refusal to see another facet of knowledge and supports the feeding of fear. The real danger lies in the darkness created by the concealment of knowledge.

Nowadays, there is a bundle of religions, although God/ universal consciousness is ONE. Wasn't the purpose to make people live in constant fear of punishment and eternal fire? Hasn't it divided us enough and turned us against each other because we don't belong to a certain religion? Haven't enough crimes been committed in the name of religion, whatever it is? Where do religions preach the love? Or the equivalent of love in this selfish world is translated by the religion of a selfish god or the god "money"?! True love does not mean murder, war, bloodshed and money.

We are said to be made in the image and likeness of a god/ goddess, so we each have the divine spark within us, and yet according to most religions we are all sinners and most condemned to eternal punishment. Isn't a god who builds his power on the knees of the many just a selfish power? Or as Jamie King (15) says, if we were able to prove that Jesus was also just a simple man, wouldn't the church and all its claims become just a fraud in its own interest and a means of manipulating the masses of people?

Along with religion, politics is another facet of mass control. It is the one that quenches its selfish thirst for power and wealth from laws that are only on paper, from divisions of nations and peoples, races, religions, division into rich and poor, into educated and illiterate, and with human sacrifices on the altar of power... Feeding fear, hatred, anger, all that is negative in the mass of the many, to their advantage, of the few, who possess the ancient knowledge of which humanity was deprived, or as W. W. Atkinson (38) says, the few who possess the knowledge and who are not suspected by the ignorant.

Knowledge can be beneficial or harmful depending on how it is used. In addition to wars, there are also viruses created in laboratories and poisons in our food. Fluoride, a byproduct of aluminium production, is added to water as the easiest way to get rid of it. When combined with the emotional manipulation led by mass media, it creates the best "dough" of humanity, chained by fear, to be controlled and manipulated.

Placing belief in something or someone outside of oneself can make one feel weak and powerless. You begin to see yourself without power. Believing in others more than in yourself, your "truth", vs. your power, becomes their "food". Furthermore, fear begets fear, the most powerful "weapon" used against humanity. However, as I said in The Recipe for Happiness (45), fear is only an illusion, that the mind gives birth to. Every idea is dissected, and divided, takes you down another path and makes the ego more powerful. It only depends on us if we permit it and accept to continue living as before or get out of the prison of fear.

All the negative information that defines our knowledge of the mind can be overcome by walking the path to knowing the wisdom of the soul, that is, trusting intuition, in what leads us back to inner harmony and harmony with nature. (12)

With or without degrees, with the rights of a slave or a king, we are all brought here on earth to learn the lessons of love. In the journey we take (if we choose) to self, we understand that true happiness does not lie in a job, money, religion or political placards. It was and is all the time within ourselves.

Limiting yourself to what the mouth of the world says, what is handed to you on a silver platter by those who have their reasons to keep you in a comfort zone and ignorance, and what the mass media offers for true brainwashing, you prefer to remain where you are. You look for quick ways to get rich, often through dishonest ways, which even if you don't admit it, deep down, you won't be proud of, and sometimes you live or end up living with deep regrets.

Believe in yourself; the power is within you. Following your intuition, the wisdom that comes from within, you feel good, you feel happy. The decision to know and use the knowledge is within your control. The way is provided by the balance that needs to be brought back to the heart and mind, a balance that we need to become creators of the life we want. It is the path of the wisdom of each of us and it lies within our soul. It does not need evidence visible to the naked eye to believe in intuition. He does not need the confirmation of others or false miracles from the religious institutions. You know that you are a miracle of creation and in turn you are a creator.

When your mind is filled with doubts and reasons not to act, your soul will simply urge you to carry on. While the mind creates '"monsters", the soul embodies the inherent wisdom it carries from the source. Believe in the unseen, and you will realize that your power lies within you, in the equilibrium between the wisdom of the soul and the knowledge of the mind. You "know" that anything is possible. Many before me have said it, and everyone has embarked on their own journey, which opens to you when you decide to change yourself."

On this journey, you will encounter the people and information needed to quench your thirst for knowledge. Whether you stumble and rise again or wait for others to help you up, understand that no one is obligated to do so. Those who are guided by their inner wisdom offer the opportunity to share their path and teach you how they lift themselves up. It is up to you to decide what to do with the knowledge offered, because as Lao Tze said, "The great man cherishes greatness, not the trivial; he seeks in mind the fruit, not the flower; he ignores this and joins the fruit" (disregarded the external and goes straight for the essence). (18)

Even if you live in fear and are surrounded by selfish actions, it does not mean that you have no right to knowledge or that you are stupid. Your power to know is not tied to a saviour outside of you. So don't expect someone to drop something into your mind and heart. You are the only one who can knock on the door of your soul "Knock and it will be opened". You are the one who has to believe in yourself, "believe and do not search". Your only salvation comes from inside, from your soul, which never lies to you. To access its wisdom, you must be the one who needs to open its gate.

*See your soul as a teacher in the discipline of love, a teacher who is always present. It always gives you the wisdom you need, while your mind gives you thoughts and solutions for what you want. You choose how you use both the knowledge of your mind and the wisdom and wealth of your soul. You might think that life knows only one meaning - forward and no one lives more experiences than they need to learn their lessons on the way back to what he is made from - **love.***

Energy and vibration

We cry and wonder why we live life the way we do, but we continue to have expectations and confirmation from others, even though life is ours. Thoughts, feelings, and actions belong to us and thus, as Okakura Kakuzo says, "we only see our own image in the universe, - our own idiosyncrasies dictate the way we perceive"(29), that is, we project what we have inside us into the world.

Everything that exists is energy, be it a tree, flower, bird or animal. We are pure energy that possesses information, energy that is stored and transmitted through our DNA, called genetic "chip" by J. J. Servan Schreiber (16). Thoughts and emotions are energy and each has its own level of vibration, and science has shown that they influence us by altering our DNA, which in turn alters the outside world through the quantum field.

Living permanently in the earth's energy field, we are continuously affected by it. The pulse emanating from the centre of our galaxy and received by the sun is transmitted to the earth. It is taken up by the heart and transmitted to the brain and to all the cells of the body. The energy of the heart influences not only our body but also the world around us. If this energy runs its course intact, our being is in flow with the universe. Conversely, if this route is interrupted by negative emotions, man is disconnected from the earth and the universe.

The Earth's pulse or Earth's magnetic resonance vibrates at the same frequency as our hearts and brain waves. Realized by Nikola Tesla in 1899, resonance was discovered by the German physicist W. O. Schumann in 1954 and named the Resonance Frequency (or Schumann Frequency). This remained at a rate of about 7.8 Hz (or cycles per second) starting to accelerate after 2012, when it increased from 7.83 Hz to the current 40.3 Hz. The peak was in 2017 when it increased from 7.83 to 36 Hz. The bottom line? Earth feels. Energy is consciousness and it cannot be destroyed, it transforms, and increasing the frequency of our thoughts and emotions means expanding the field of consciousness. Furthermore, due to the electromagnetic field, it is only natural that what we send out into the universe is what we will receive.

That everything is in motion and vibrates, and nothing is at rest was known to the scholars of ancient Egypt and was summarised in the Principle of Vibration in the Kybalion, which says that "Everything is in motion, everything vibrates, nothing is at rest" (39). The principle works on a cosmic scale, it exists in the history of all things, whether they are suns, worlds, animals, plants or people, whether we are talking about the rise and fall of nations or the mental states of people, "From the corpuscle to the electron, from the atom to molecule to worlds and universes, everything moves, everything vibrates". (39)

For centuries, this knowledge was ignored and lost sight of by thinkers. Since the 19th century, science has rediscovered the truth and added additional evidence to it (39).

W. W. Atkinson (38) explains vibration as "a state of intense and rapid movement of a particle", and the difference lies in the frequency of the vibration. Whether we're talking about quantum physics and superstring theory or M-theory, they all tell us that everything that exists is made up of tiny circular strings that have different vibrational frequencies (25). Waves are felt as vibrations of a medium that supports them, says Fritoj Kapra in Theophysics (12). Waves are water vibrations, sounds are air vibrations. The differences that exist between the modes of manifestation of matter, energy, soul and spirit are given by differences in vibration.

If according to classical physics (12), mass was seen as a material substance and conserved like energy, the theory of relativity shows us that mass is only a form of energy that can be condensed into the form of the mass of an object. Objects at rest store energy in the form of mass and the connection is given by the theory of relativity (E=mc2).

Adherents of Eastern philosophy see the Universe as a living network, whose connections are not static, but dynamic, and the dynamic is one of the most important aspects of this philosophy, says Fritoj Kapra (12). Being alive, the cosmic network is in movement, development and continuous change. Symbol of the dynamics of the Universe, of the flow of energy that takes an infinity of forms that melt into one another, is also the dance of the god Shiva. The dynamic character of the Universe is also recognized by modern physics, which sees it like Eastern philosophy, as a network in continuous movement, as a cosmic dance of energy, which is not chaotic but follows clear and well-defined schemes.

*Have you ever thought about someone and then shortly after that person called you? Or texted you or met him? Have you ever felt someone staring at you even though your back is turned? They are not coincidences. They are due to **the morphic fields** that coordinate the vibratory activity of the nervous system and are related to mental activity. Through them, minds are extended beyond the brain, and the effects of attention and intention at a distance can be detected experimentally, says Dr Rupert Sheldrake, speaking about "Morphogenetic Fields of Body and Mind" (42), in a presentation from the online event, World Summit of Integrative Medicine 2015. It is also through the morphic fields that the morphic resonance works giving the inherent memory to any self-organizing system, including crystals, plants, and animals.*

*Through the inherent memory which is genetic memory, also known as ancestral memory, certain memories, knowledge or traits can be inherited or transmitted from one generation to another through mechanisms (genetic or epigenetic) that seem to be interconnected in the process of evolution and predisposition to disease, and at the same time they involve the storage and transmission of information in an organism's DNA. But **this information does not only mean biological traits, but also emotional and psychological legacies.** The child becomes the bearer of unresolved traumas and the "basket" of the parents' aspirations. Therefore, human beings rely on collective memory, but at the same time, contribute to it.*

Another example that gives us the image of interconnectivity is the one provided by Dan Farcaş (8), known to electrography researchers, namely that the aura "expresses" what two people feel, towards each other, when they bring their hands together.

Their auras merge in the case of sympathy or repel in the case of hostility.

Interconnectivity exists in nature. Plants recognize their neighbours, their families, and strangers. Therefore, they sometimes slow down their growth to favour others or grow faster to occupy the land. Climbing plants do not look for support points at random, but feel them even if there are obstacles in their way.

Among other examples provided by Dan Farcaș (8), there is the research done during the communist period by a team led by Marioara Godeanu and D. Constantin that showed that poisoning a plant with mercury sulfate led to an increase in temperature not only of the respective plant but also of the related neighbour, and "arms of energy" were noticed that the healthy plant extended to the sick one as if to help.

*C. Backster's experiments related to lie detectors led to the finding that plants react with simple harming intentions. Through the research done by Thelma Moss, it was observed that plants react to the intentions with which man approaches them. Thus, aggressive intentions almost erase the plant's aura, as if robbing it; and approaching it with good thoughts makes the plant's aura amplify. James Redfield's book, **The Celestine Prophecies**, or the movie of the same name, captures this energetic rapprochement between humans, and between humans and nature.*

Beyond all of the above, many of us witness cats and dogs waiting for us at the entrance when we return home because they know, they feel when we return.

Thus, our world is a world in which everything is interconnected, or as Fritoj Kapra (12) says, a world of constant rhythm, movement and transformation, in which everything follows clear laws. Every thought, every emotion and every state of mind has its vibrational degree. These mental states can be reproduced just as it is possible to reproduce a musical sound by making a musical instrument vibrate in a certain way, or as a colour can be reproduced to make an object vibrate.

All particles of matter vibrate and are in motion. Molecules are made of atoms, atoms of corpuscles. All are in a constant state of vibration and movement. Every thought affects the entire world and impacts the whole universe. The energies we emit meet similar energies, that's why certain people are attracted to our lives. When we say "I feel finished", or "I feel in the ninth heaven" we express the emotion we experience because fear is energy and vibration, as is love. The difference is in the frequency of vibration those emotions have. Everything we think and feel moment to moment is transmitted to the cosmic energy field that interacts with everything around us and everything interacts back with us. Our feelings influence our DNA and because we are interconnected, they change our world.

DNA is known to be the carrier of the genetic message. Although genes represent only 5% of DNA, the genetic information in which human individuality consists is written in every cell of the human body. The components of the DNA chains (called nucleotides) by the precise order in which they are placed, in which one chain is complementary to the other, make up a message just as letters do in a text (8). The remaining 95% of DNA, which has been called "junk", has been shown by Russian researchers to be used in our vast process of communication with others, which leaves its mark on those around us and the entire world.

Being energy, we emit and store light. It is not for nothing that we are told when we are angry that "you are black as the earth", and when we are happy or when we love, that we are radiant, that we are bright. Our state of mind is read in our eyes and face. The more energy, and light we have, the brighter, the more positive we are.

It is DNA that energizes us in the body's regeneration process, cell by cell, sends light through blood, organs and neural networks through information, and morphic fields **organize** *bodies through vibration and can aid healing. Every cell of the body contains memory, or as Patricia Cori says, there is a mind in every cell of the body, in every subatomic particle and in the DNA of all beings (32).*

Experiments done to test the influence of our emotions on DNA have shown that regardless of the location of a subject and the DNA samples collected from that subject, placed at a distance of hundreds of km, the emission of emotion by that subject and the reaction of the DNA occurred simultaneously, as if the DNA were in the subject's body, because it perceives everything we feel and think in less than a nanosecond (billionth of a second/ 0.000000001 sec). Furthermore, if one of the DNA strands is damaged, it can replicate after the nucleotides on the paired strand (8).

Everything that happens to each of us is determined by our own vibration (32). Experiencing anger, hatred, and stress, the strands of our DNA shrink, contract and block many of its codes. There is what Alice Miller (1) calls "emotional blindness" that produces barriers to protect us against trauma. Although they belong to the past, they remain encoded in the brain as a permanent danger. The body has the memory of the emotions experienced and although it has no voice, it speaks to us in its own language, through all kinds of signs to attract our attention. Moreover, because he knows everything that has happened to him, we unconsciously pass on to the next generation the harm that we have suffered. The blockages in us stop us from assimilating new information and make it difficult or impossible for us to escape the repetition of evil. Thus, it is common that in fear, anger, anxiety, and depression we feel isolated from the rest of the world, but we isolate ourselves with what we have stored inside us and sent out into the universe.

The brain does not know who you blame and criticize. It does not know who you wish harm to and takes personally what you "think" you give to others because the subconscious mind does not relate to anyone or anything. It makes no difference between you and others. It does not differentiate between giving and receiving. It doesn't care if your feelings are false or true. It always accepts as your truth, what you feel is true, and you are what you believe. It takes everything you give to. What you give, is what you get, because you "can't give what you don't have and you only have what you believe." (27)

If the Hawaiians believed that both the heart and the brain had their own wisdom, for the ancient Egyptians the heart was the source of it and the centre of emotions, being the most important of the internal organs and they acted accordingly. That is, the embalmers had the task of preparing the mummification, extracting and removing the moist parts of the body. The most important ones were buried with the mummy, i.e. the heart and intestines, while the brain was thrown away because it was not considered important. Schopenhauer (5) calls the heart the centre of the body and the symbol of the will, and the brain follows. That is why, he says, a hero's heart is embalmed, while philosophers and poets have their brains searched after death.

In "The Day I Learned to Love Myself" Laurent Gounelle talks about the animals that fled before the seismic wave of 2004, about the elephants that no longer obeyed commands and about thousands of people from primitive tribes who escaped with their lives just because they followed their intuition by listening to nature (19).

We humans, without following our intuition, are like a compass without a needle. We are gifted with everything we need, but we do not believe in ourselves and our soul guide. In our society, the use of reason has been promoted, that's why, in power, is the expression "think, that's why you have a brain!" Usually, we also use the expressions "he is heartless", he has a big heart", "he has a cold heart", and "my heart bursts with joy", on the other hand, I have not heard it said "have a heart, listen to it!". We were not taught to listen to our intuition, or in many cases where we did, we were punished under the idea, "you don't live from the heart". By valuing the mind, we have lost touch with intuition, and our nature, because by allowing ourselves to be led by the outside, we give it our power and follow our reason by crushing intuition.

We are told about the neurons in the brain. But the neurons in the heart? Having long and short-term memory, the signals sent by its neurons to the brain influence our emotional experience. The heart has its own electromagnetic field that sends signals to the brain. At the Institute of the Heartmath, they measured the amplitude of brain waves and heart waves and found that the electromagnetic field of the heart is 5000 times stronger than that of the brain, and the energy changes according to the emotions emitted, not our thoughts. Send fear, you will experience those things you fear, send love, receive love. The law of cause and effect is irreversible. Thinking that your life has no meaning, it will be that way, because fears guide you. Desires from the soul become real, and our healing is possible, out of love. What you believe is based on what you vibrate and is what you will experience.

By trying to live a different life through the prism of past hurts, you will manifest the events that have filled your life until now, because your filters are set on fear and its weapons. It's like when I need to reinstall an app on my laptop and have to delete the old one so the new version can take its place. In a way, I let go of it, everything that I no longer had the opportunity to use. It is something similar to what happens to our power. To return to the original setting, to unconditional love, it is necessary to let go of the settings made by fear and return to the wealth of the soul. This is where some people's "luck" comes from and others' bad luck, and to change the frequency of what you live to what you want to live, David Icke's advice (9) is to open your heart and mind, to reconnect to the source of infinite power.

Each of us creates our own reality and carries it with us, driven by its vibration. No one in our external world is to blame for what we experience, because only we are responsible for our thoughts and emotions. "There is no influence outside of (man's) mind." (27)

Everything that is emotion has as its source of our thinking and we too can free ourselves from negative emotions. Consciously accepting them, they will no longer be experienced. They disappear taking with them that inner pain you felt in their presence. All that you have stored in yourself, which you carry with you and in vain you throw the blame on others because the baggage is yours, there can be no others to blame. In addition, with the release of emotions, you will feel lighter. It's not fantasy, not a children's story. Emotions take up space in your body, and that space will be freed with their release, making you feel freer, lighter, and happier. And then, who do you want to be responsible for you and your happiness? Because many prefer to live as they did and as they know, they are repeating what their ancestors did. To get out of the blockages it is necessary to discover their origin in our own childhood because no matter how much we avoid them, emotional traumas are present in us and the past continuously follows us in all the relationships we have, with our peers or with our children. If on the one hand, we can see them as beneficial because they protect us from suffering, from inner pain, on the other hand, they are toxic because we unconsciously harm ourselves and others.

Changing negative emotions into love and gratitude clears blockages, and love and gratitude, also bring physiological benefits to our body, helping our DNA to expand (its chains open and grow). Positive emotions also help us to be creative and to find solutions in solving problems.

Our condition also influences the water contained in our bodies. It is known that water is indispensable to life, and if we don't consume enough water, the body suffers, man becoming "more or less like a dry apple", as W. W. Atkinson says (37).

Research by I. Mînzatu, from the years of communism, mentioned by Dan Farcaș (8), showed that water can also be found in the form of double-helix molecules, thus reminiscent of the DNA molecule, but while in it the spirals are twisted only to the right, those in water can be to the right or to the left, which shows its quality of being compatible with life or not. In addition, the fact that water structures exhibit spontaneous oscillations is proof that water resonates with vibrations coming from outside.

Thus, water influences our lives, and we influence it in turn because we transmit our thoughts and emotions to it, and as I said, it has memory. Dr. Masaru Emoto impregnated the distilled water crystals with the corresponding energy of different words (luck, bad luck, success, fool, safety, thank you, love) and the water molecules gave rise to varied shapes, the beauty of which depended on the vibration the word used (22). So water reacts to our thoughts and feelings, to words and images. We are 70% water, which means the influence of words on the body through their vibration.

Because we are all interconnected, we can all contribute to changing the role of water for the better in our lives and fight for healthy water on the planet. Furthermore, the words coming from the vibrations of the universe should help us see that we are all one. (22) This leads us back to the idea that there is no "I" and the rest of the world. There is no barrier between "me" and "others", everything is "I am", an infinite mind and a universal consciousness governed by the most important natural and spiritual law, the law of unconditional love.

For those looking for a scientific explanation, quantum theory has demolished the notion of an isolated object, because the world cannot be composed of entities that are independent of each other, says Fritoj Kapra (12). Just as the particle cannot be viewed in isolation, but as part of the whole, so the parts of the Universe are defined by their connections with the whole, nature is a system of relationships that unites the different parts of the whole, revealing the unity of the Universe, a reality experienced not only by mystics orientals but also by quantum theory. (12) Even in atomic physics we can no longer talk about nature without being involved, says Fritoj Kapra, because at the atomic level, the division between "I" and the world no longer works. Humanity is like an ocean, composed of us men like drops of water that all look the same and yet are different from each other.

We are interconnected and yet, often disconnected from this ocean called infinite mind or consciousness. However, every particle of this infinite mind has its share of influence in the great field of consciousness. By leaving the prison of fear you open your heart and mind and understand that you are a piece of the puzzle of the universe, you are part of the universal consciousness to which you are connected.

O moment of LOVE

We are all connected to the source from which we come, to the love of ONE. To understand this, I needed to learn the lessons that life has given me and answer the questions that haunted me since I was a small child, coming home from school crying. To the question of why there is so much selfishness, pride, and struggle for power in our world, the answer I found was confirmed by the story of another little girl, who, despite the years that have passed, remained my friend.

At the moment I remembered, she said to me:

"I know a poem. Do you want to listen to it?

Now? (I was surprised because I had planned to help her with a school project).

*Yes, please, because **nobody got time for me. Mom is always tired, and nervous and says she doesn't have time. Daddy is also tired or impatient."***

I was momentarily silent and confused. The explanations continued and flowed one after the other. I understood that she wanted to give me as many explanations as she could, afraid that I would refuse her, too. She was looking for reasons to listen to her, so that at the same time I wouldn't give her reasons to reject her. Listening to her poetry, I remembered myself and others, when I was a child/children, I asked for a moment's attention from my parents and it came too late or maybe it never came.

How many of us, being children, have not experienced such moments? How many have not seen their parents running after, to and from work, after food, after everything, but they did not find, do not find time to offer comfort, do not make time for a hug or play with the child? How many have time for friends, TV, alcohol, and drugs, but don't have time for a moment of attention/love that their child requires?

It is scientifically proven that the experiences of the first days, weeks and months of life are decisive for the structuring of the brain. Loving attention is vital to the formation of the capacity for empathy, a capacity that is lost when a child grows up in an unloving environment, says Alice Miller (1).

If we look at ourselves through the angle of the society we live in, with angry people, who are always looking to achieve, to get rich, to accumulate more and more, a society where violence is always looking to break out in every corner of life, and frustration is in power, we can ask "How many people have received their moment of love?"

*Those repeated moments, in which a child is not given the required attention, explanations that he asks directly or indirectly, and the satisfaction of the need for communication, affection, and interaction at his level, will cause him to sediment and grow false worthlessness. He will grow up believing that he is not good enough to be loved if even his parents do not have time to give him what he is asking for - a moment of love. True, the child does not know that money is needed, he knows that he wants a hug that he longs for, a smile from his mother, and encouragement from his father. How many have not deprived their child of that moment of love that he longed for, thinking that he has money, clothes food, he has a phone and a new game ... so, he **is loved**? It's just that satisfying physiological needs doesn't equate to emotional needs, and we're basically emotions. Moreover, childhood trauma destroys existing neurons as well as newly formed ones by producing stress hormones, says Alice Miller, which is shown by the existence of lesions in the areas of the brain that control emotions, damage that, according to neurobiology studies, can reach a third of the brain.*

The child accepts or rejects a stranger at first sight. He respects without rational thought, what he feels, because he is pure

LOVE. That bit of love that wasn't given, in the past, may be considered vital by a child's soul, but it can be so insignificant to an adult who knows they don't have time or have better things to do than "waste time" listening to a story, a poem, or playing a little with his child because he, in turn, didn't get his moment of love either.

The negative emotion of rejection that the child experiences at that moment, that there is no time for him, or that he probably did something bad, becomes in time a frustration. As a teenager, it deepens, and as an adult, he can live a life with it. It can be the spring that will become an ocean of pain in which to swim for a lifetime. In the depths of his soul, he will know that "I cannot be loved, I cannot be worthy, I am not good, I cannot do anything by myself and I must look for someone or something to be mine, to know myself loved". He will look outside of himself for everything that was not offered to satisfy the need for love that he felt inside. It's just that what is forced from the outside will not be good for the child's brain, because it needs its own rhythm of stimulation, says Alice Miller (1).

*From the lack of the moment of love, failed relationships, toxic loves, repressed pain, addictions, depression, rivers of tears, searching for love in other forms just to please others, to give and receive a proof that it can be... **loved**.*

Somewhere, deep in my soul, I know that when I listened to that girl's poetry, I gave her the touch of love that she wanted. Confirmation was given to me by the smile that bloomed on her bright face and the happiness reflected in her eyes. Thus, for my part, I received gratitude for that moment I gave her by listening to that poem. Is a drop of love really expensive?

What we give is what we get. Some say it is the coincidence of things. However, in our world, there is no such thing. The universe does not work on coincidences, but on the laws that govern it. We experience the results of our feelings and thoughts. Everything we offer today, builds what we will receive in another day of "today", which we call the future. Changing the frequency of our thoughts by offering positivity even when we don't receive it is another way to shape our world to look different. It seems difficult, but each of us can do it with and from love.

On the path of selfishness, I believed that good must come back from the person to whom I did good, and that evil works the same way. But the blows that life has given me, have taught me that you can experience bad where you least expect it and good to come from the person you least expect or you never thought you would - will provide it. This is because as I said, the law of cause and effect of the universe does not take into account the person, but the thoughts that you send out into the universe. They return to you with a tenfold, therefore, we cannot be surprised at the world in which we live.

Each of us came to this planet to become better and to learn to love by giving love to others without expecting rewards. They will come anyway because the laws of the universe work the same way for everyone.

We can have "everything", but if we use the weapons of fear and selfishness, we will not find happiness and spiritual joy. When we start cleaning through our emotions we open the door of the soul. Thus we can understand that we cannot change the past, but we can change the way we see things and our reactions to understand them and fully accept ourselves as we are. It is said that then the heart chakra opens, which aligns with the cosmic pulse of the earth, the sun, the galaxy (9).

The decision to choose to continue living in the prison of fear or in the freedom of love belongs to each of us.

2. Mind and Obstacles

Take your life as granted. Not to hit it, but to better hear its heart beat.

Tudor Mușatescu (44)

Throughout my life I have often had the feeling that I was experiencing the same events repeatedly, only that each time, next to me as the main character, there were always other characters, and all happened in different times and places.

From my collection of memories, I recall the Carpathian Mountains, many tourists, and a narrow path. "I find myself crouching on the steep path, gazing into the abyss on my right. Fear grips me, rendering me immobile. I feel stuck, unable to move up or down. In an instant, all other thoughts vanish, leaving only one: the source of my paralysis is my fear of death. I know that a single misstep driven by this fear would be fatal. My fate would be sealed in the gaping chasm beside me.

The world seems frozen in time. The few tourists nearby all stand still and watch. I can feel my breathing making noise. From below, I suddenly hear my child's voice "Mom, I'm coming to get you". "No!", I answered, calculating in a fraction of a second that I would rather die if my life was meant to end there, but I will not put my child's life in danger. I realize that the decision to go up or down is mine and I take the risk that comes with it. No one moves, everyone waits to see what happens next. With my decision made, I get up and turn around. Then I follow another path. It all takes a few seconds, but I know they were among the most difficult of my life." (46)

Moments of fear, like the one above, I experienced because I had not yet fully accepted the knowledge of the soul, still guiding myself much by reason. Thus, I was looking for solutions to what the outside world offered me. Starting to ask myself more and more questions why the same thing happens to me, I began to see that beyond everything that is shown to me with my physical eyes, there is also another world, within us from which we create what we live. I began to understand what a great enemy I was to myself because I was relying on fear. The more I asked myself "Why am I afraid?", "What if I still try...?" "What do I have to lose?", "Don't I have more to gain?", I started to receive more and more information, in all kinds of ways: I heard certain lyrics on the radio, and certain book titles or quotes appeared on the Internet pages I used to visit. From each, I took and accepted the answers that I felt resonated with my inner truth.

In this way, I understood that nothing I experienced was accidental. What I was doing or saying was no mere accident. I understood that others were not responsible for my choices, because only I made them, based on the baggage I carried inside me. They were the result of the way I thought and lived, the result of my self-image. The mind, what we call our reason, is the self-image, and everything beyond it, attracts or frightens us, says Carlos Castaneda (6).

Unconsciously we use expressions like "it's hard", "it's difficult", "it's not possible", "it has to", and "it's terrible", which have a very low connotation and reflect the world we live in, but it's the world we create it and we do it for ourselves. We rely on what we know from lived experiences, from what others offer us as facts who may or may not be interested in seeing another side of things, but without looking for that, without trying to act differently than we did until then, it will be hard to believe in ourselves. By always doing everything we've done before, without trying anything else, without satisfying our curiosity, we have no way to live anything other than what we've lived up to that moment. Only when life brings you to a crossroads and you go lower than you thought you could go, you look for the solution to get you out of the impasse.

What you say or do in life is not accidental. In fact, we believe in difficulty because we do not know or believe that we have the courage to act and go in a different direction than we have done before. Fear of risk, fear of new, fear of beginning, fear of death, explode inside us and make us retreat from a new path, to continue walking the same beaten path for years or even a lifetime, a path we are comfortable with. We allow our fears to take over and lead us in their direction.

When we don't even accept to learn about another facet of things, it's because our selfishness thinks "I know it all". It's just that we only rely on what we've learned up to that point from our own experiences and what others have offered us as "absolute truth", and we've taken them for granted. However, no one owns the absolute truth, we each own only our own truth born of our thoughts and emotions.

*Accepting to learn about other people's truths, that is, to see other sides of things, does not mean believing in them. It doesn't mean changing the ideas you believe in. This is our only reason for not doing it. **We are AFRAID that what we will learn about ourselves might shake our confidence in what we knew until then. It means we fear the truth of others because of what might come out of ourselves.***

We can get to know another side of things by asking questions, reading and looking for answers even where we think we won't find them, even where we don't like to look for them. Fragments of answers come from everywhere and together form a picture that we often don't want to know or believe exists, especially inside us. But traumas exist, live within us, and have shaped our identity. They are alive, even though they are from the past. We carry them with us and relive them over and over again until we are tired of experiencing them and learn our lessons.

Even though they have shaped us, they do not define us, and we can rewrite the script of life without what our ancestors experienced and did not process or understand and pass on to us. We break unresolved emotional loops and patterns rooted in the unspoken legacies of generations and decide to follow our path in a different way than it has been done before us. We find our wholeness and reveal our uniqueness.

Trauma is based on fear and causes us to doubt ourselves, our abilities, and our power to create the life we want. The fear in our mind is what makes us swallow the illusion that "living is difficult", because it becomes an obstacle in the functioning, but also in man's healing. The remedy is, states W. W. Atkinson, the removal of the obstacles any man has built up through his own fears. (37)

It's easy to find reasons not to do certain things. With the belief that you are not good, and valuable, you look for reasons to put curiosity aside, and with it, you will give up another facet of knowledge, and some choose to give up on life.

It's even easier to blame others, especially if they live the way they like. Instead, it's hard to do what you want on your own. It's hard to thank yourself, it's hard to appreciate yourself and others. It's hard to apologise, it's hard... even to live. However, at the end of a critical situation, many of us say that we have passed "this trouble", this problem, that life goes on and we say that anything considered difficult can be overcome. Things are hard because we haven't looked for a solution or found it yet. However, by crying, we don't even find a solution, but we wait for others to offer us mercy, compassion and solutions.

Just as a whole is made up of small pieces together, difficulty can be seen as a whole puzzle that needs a beginning. The most difficult is to fix the first pieces, and then the others all follow in turn, and each in its place. Everything can be done piece by piece, or following the advice of René Descartes, let's divide each difficulty into as many parts as possible and necessary to find its solution (44). Each part of the whole needs attention to put it in its place in the whole we want, understanding that not everything can be solved at once.

Every step taken despite what we see as difficult, is taken to ease the problem. Any small aspect that may seem insignificant is just a piece of the puzzle of that problem. The whole is made of details, right? Solving one problem brings the solution to other problems, and the weight keeps getting smaller. In the end, it comes to the idea that difficulty is only an illusion that separates us from a result.

We can take steps step by step and remember that any solution also involves risks. By assuming them, we become responsible for ourselves, for our lives and for the world we live in. Looking back at everything we have experienced, we can understand that any difficulty once solved seems easier. We feel good about ourselves for having found the solution, for as Publius Syrus says, "the sweetest pleasure comes from overcoming difficulties." (44)

It seems hard to believe, but sometimes the solution is right under our noses, in some cases the very thing we see as a problem, may be the solution. The only limits are the ones we impose on ourselves out of the belief "it is difficult".

Thinking within the walls built by fear, you will create an obstacle course accompanied by pain and bitter tears. You unconsciously limit yourself to obstacles, living like a mere dreamer. Your dreams remain in the "unfulfilled dreams" file for various reasons, and obstacles sought by the mind, and without dreams, we become machines. Moreover, with "broken dreams", you don't feel good or you feel like you have no reason to live. You can let them sleep for the rest of your life and consider that you are simply comfortable in the world you live in and don't care if you live or not your way. However, most of the time life does not end with a shattered dream, with a failure. You can choose to start over. With free thinking, the limits you consciously impose on yourself, you enter into harmony with your soul, your body, and the whole earth. As a creator, you see no obstacles, only reasons to get up and move on, regardless of who is with you or not.

How many dreams have you allowed to become real, to be part of the reality you live in? How many have you killed out of fear of... You can change your dreams into reality or you can throw them in the bottom of your soul, hide them to remain simply dreams. Killed from the very beginning, some of them are lost in time, and you will say that you are unhappy. But your unhappiness comes from your fear of facing them and taking action. It is no one's fault if they remain only dreams or if we agree with others that our dreams are too small or too big. They have no dimension because there are no important dreams and unimportant dreams. You are the one who gives them dimension, whether or not you allow them to become real. They are unique as we are, but your fear, your lack of confidence in yourself and your powers, make you stay chained or lose opportunities offered by life events, and sometimes lose the battle to do what you want.

By looking honestly within yourself, you will see you have many dreams. They are part of you, of your being and they become reality as long as you believe in yourself, believe in them and take action in that direction as Neville Goddard says "Any dream could be achieved by those self-disciplined enough to believe it. [...] Let us, therefore, always be prepared; otherwise, we either lose an opportunity or lose the battle."(27)

We can use the opportunities that come our way, to make changes that not many are willing to make. The reasons can be diverse from the lack of pleasure that they complicate their lives, to the desire not to feel the pain inside them. They feel that change can complicate their lives, or they look for others to support them and if possible fight their own battles. Sometimes they look for and follow other paths to quick results, paths I have called the weapons of fear.

Regardless of how many obstacles you will find in your path, they are all for "your good". It seems hard to believe, but without obstacles, we will not see how far we are willing to go and how much we want certain things. No matter how much you hide or hide your fears from yourself, at some point you will have to face the monsters born of fear. If you're living the way I've lived many times, waiting for someone to support me in my dreams, I can tell you're afraid of something. Whenever you don't act on your heart, you find yourself regretting not doing it. You know things you've always known, but if you don't have faith in yourself and your power, it's hard to start, it's hard to act, and you feel it's hard to finish something. You can find a lot of reasons not to do anything for your dreams because "it's hard" and you "can't".

If you listen to your soul, which never lies, it knows that anything is possible. It is the only voice you can trust, and always knows which way to go, because inside your heart is your truth, a truth of your uniqueness, and authenticity. Feeling, believing and following your intuition/soul is how you can overcome your fears.

In the book "Recipe for Happiness" (45) I said that I also lived for years with the idea that "when.... I will do and I will have", or as Lise Bourbeau (20) says, when I have a certain thing I will be in a position to be able to act, and thus be happy. I was conditioning myself. It's just that life offered me many lessons from which I could learn that everything comes and goes and that all we have is just the moment we are in, the present, called by Irvin D. Yalom "a moment in the sun" (14). The rest, a part has become the past and it is history, a part is a "mystery" that will be lived someday in what we call the future, but prepared by us now, in the present.

Together, the memories of the past and the wishes that look to the future only disturb the peace that we can live in the present. To believe in the past is to live in the past. Believing in a future means that you want to live in a moment that you don't know when it will come or if it will ever come. Both variants prove the lack of faith in us and in our inner strength. Both become obstacles in our minds based on the emotion of fear that we allow to rule our lives. Born from what is instilled in our minds from an early age, fear will increase through education received and experiences lived in everyday life. Living with the idea that it is a sin to appeal to the curiosity of knowledge and that you are "good" if you only do what you are told, you no longer tend to seek to find out the causes of evil in yourself, and you give up looking for your good.

In our opinion about reality, the reason that characterizes us, says Dan Farcaş (8), is located at the top of the mental hierarchy, dominates and acquires the power of law, even if the sense organs say something completely different. This is because the conscious mind controls the human mind. Once the verbal top of the pyramid of the human mind is convinced, the subordinate entities will cooperate, play along and often silence the voice of intuition. It's just that our nature is intuition, that divine part of us, so Taoism sees reasoning as part of the false world that is created by man, from which moral standards and social etiquette are born. Therefore, its path and that of Hinduism and Buddhism aim at liberation from the power of reason, from the limitations and relativity of rational thought (12).

The mind knows what we have experienced and is constantly looking for reason in what is happening, and the attached emotions are what we call upon to take action. Allowing fear to take over our lives, the mind will look for solutions based on the doubts and they give us other fears, and doubts in turn. We are spinning in a labyrinth from which some end up in depression or end their own lives. The mind trapped in the prison of fear becomes an obstacle to our life, taking precedence over the heart. It treads on the heart. Therefore, for years or a whole life we feel suffering, burdened, unhappy, dissatisfied, living with a "heavy heart".

When you follow a different path than the one that most people follow, i.e. when you follow your intuition, you hear expressions like "there is no such thing", "this is not possible", "there is no way you can succeed in this ". How does anyone else know what I want? Have they lived my truth? Does they know my insides to know what I resonate with?

Our thoughts attract the vibrations we resonate with. Considering yourself powerless, and weak, you will attract people and events that will confirm you are weak. Living with the thought that you cannot do something because you are under the control of others, you will have those experiences that show you that you cannot do anything without that control. The experiences you will live will show you that you are and have what you believe, that is, you have no power and no control over your life, and the sum of our decisions born from negative thoughts and emotions, define our "hell". It is the punishment we give ourselves unconsciously for what we have stored within. No one and nothing else does. You are the one punishing yourself as long as you live chained in the prison of fear.

From this position it is comfortable for you to strongly believe, listen and follow the wishes or will of those you see as stronger than you, that is, you give your power to external causes, which according to what is written in the Kybalion (39), do nothing but it directs you to play the game of life as a mere pawn at the hands of those with stronger wills and desires than yours, and thus you live without making much use of your masculine principle (39). You live the effects of the environment instead of becoming your own cause, and the fault of the thoughts and emotions you have is not even yours. They only translate reality for you. The guilt you may be throwing behind others has another owner you don't want or don't know how to acknowledge: the baggage inside you.

To become the master of your life and not a pawn, you will need to take responsibility for that baggage and look for its causes. You are the only one who can break the chains of fear, heal the wounds and start building the "heaven" you want. Only you can rise above the effects of outside influences and become the centre of your own universe. Lifting the veil of fears, you step over them and believe in yourself, in your intuition. Following it, you don't think about how many obstacles you will encounter, you don't think about how hard it will be, you only take action.

Also out of fear, it's hard to start something new, different from what you've done so far, but "appetite comes with eating". The first time you will take action with fear. The second time you'll think it was hard the first time, so now it can't be harder than it was in the beginning. The next steps will become easier and slowly, slowly, you get used to the fact that life can be lived differently, without fear. Additionally, everything you do is overcoming fear. It will increase your self-confidence, self-esteem, and self-respect, and thus, you will learn to love yourself.

Every thought is energy and is born in the unseen, invisible world. Also there, in our mind, we create its mental image. The more we think about it, the more we become attached to the thought, but the energy that will support it can be beneficial or harmful to us. It will be beneficial when we think about that thing, but the emotion that will accompany it will be one of joy, pleasure and at the same time detachment, regardless of the result obtained; "whether it is fulfilled or not, it's good anyway, because "I remain myself". It is as if we believe in that unseen force to create our desires, and the Universe does its work for everyone according to its laws.

At the opposite pole is the other variant, when we live our lives based on the emotional patterns stored in our subconscious. They will influence our lives in any field because the subconscious is like a computer that has stored every moment of our existence. It holds the key to those emotions with all the details about them. From this position, the mental image we create is accompanied by suffering if it is not realized. The idea of not being fulfilled makes us feel small, weak, and powerless, we will resort to cowardice, praise, and conceit. The thought that we will prove to others who we are, makes us feel important and special, but it is based on fears and pride, on selfishness.

Every wish that comes true comes only at the right time and place in our lives because, as Neville Goddard says, "All men have the power to create reality, but this power sleeps as if dead when not exercised. People live in the very heart of creation - the Human Imagination - and yet they do not have the wisdom to notice what is going on inside." (26)

It is said that our soul is tied with a "string" to the source we come from. This means that the love that guides us in our desires and dreams is all connected to the "central" source. We become creators of what exists around us and have our contribution or fault in everything we experience as humanity. As I said, we are each a drop in the water of its ocean, because we are each a piece in the puzzle of humanity. We are co-creators of this world, whether we like it or not.

Returning to obstacles, rational thinking becomes an obstacle in the life we want because we want to believe "if we see with our own eyes". We condition our thoughts. "I would like to, but I don't have..." is the most common phrase with which we block our thoughts alone. "I can't/you can't, because I don't have it", and "I can't/you can't, because..." are expressions with which we discourage ourselves and others discourage you from doing what we want and believe. The reason you do it is your fears. Others' motives are related to the belief that their version is the best, that their truth is superior to your truth. It is the version offered by their reason, born from their perceptions and experiences, and you follow that version because you don't believe in yourself, you don't see yourself as good enough, and you don't look for your own versions born from your feelings or you don't believe in them.

You also create obstacles when you limit the resolution of any event to a single solution, which may not have met your expectations. You don't consider other paths the universe offers you because you are afraid to open other doors that appear in your path. You don't even want to peek to see what lies beyond them. You have not come into contact with other information, and yet it does not seem conclusive to you, because you do not have visible confirmation or it is not provided by those you trust, that it will be fine, that you will succeed. Without such confirmation, you feel lost.

Our mind becomes an obstacle to the life we want because of the rigid beliefs we live with. We model ourselves after them until we come to identify with them and to overcome the obstacles of the mind, thoughts need to be freed from these beliefs. They need to leave the prison and free themselves from their fears. Releasing negative emotions will release the thoughts that accompany them. You will know pain, because only when you "eat pain on bread" (as my son says) can you descend into the greatest darkness within you. Only then and there you face the biggest demons you have locked up within you. By waging your inner war with them, you will think freely, connected to the infinite mind. Space will be created within you for positive emotions. Then the mind will be devoted to the heart and all that it signifies.

Returning to the solutions we seek for what we experience, to dwell only on what we see with our physical eyes will only live in the world of selfishness. You limit yourself to what you see, you will be controlled by fear, becoming its slave, because between fears, the mind becomes selfish. It collects, memorises, analyses, uses reason, and knows only what it has stored up during your life. All these will be the ones that will make it an obstacle in your way as long as you do not grant the soul the right it came into this world with - to guide you. The mind can be directed by what it sees or hears from the outside, but the soul listens only to itself because it is connected to that "infinite source of consciousness".

The Garden of "selfishness"

The fear of making mistakes, expressing ourselves, speaking our minds, respecting our limits, admitting vulnerability, and feeling weak and powerless gives rise to defence mechanisms. They take various forms and perpetuate selfishness. They also develop gradually, gaining power through all experiences with the same frequency of vibration.

These defences emerge and evolve because we are punished without having our opinions heard. We are often not given the right to express our opinions or are ridiculed for our views. Additionally, we are labelled because of our mistakes, and selfishness disapproves of mistakes and punishes them. They make their way into us when our privacy is not respected; when we are not explained our mistakes and that we can learn from those mistakes; when we are not offered alternatives and are laughed at are laughed at for not dressing as well as others. Selfishness adds to its "bouquet" and grows when our achievements are not valued as much as those of others, when we work for others without receiving recognition or when our efforts are dismissed. It flourishes when our financial means are not as substantial as those of others. Finally, our selfishness becomes apparent when we take credit for others' work and boast about their results as if they were our own.

In this way, in our journey through life, we often cultivate many negative qualities within ourselves, similar to weeds in a garden. While weeds may have their uses in nature, within us, they manifest as arrogance, spite, hatred, malice, revenge, lies, flattery, and cowardice... a bundle of weeds that we grow and offer to those around us, but they define the garden of "selfishness".

Although we often claim to live in a more just society than our predecessors, those who speak candidly are often ostracised and criticised, put against the wall and stoned. This discourages many people from expressing their thoughts and taking a stand when they feel compelled to do so. We strive to conform to societal norms, even when they contradict our true beliefs and values. We blindly adhere to these norms simply because "that's how it should be, "that's good", "that's beautiful", "that's what everyone does". But "I" is not everyone, just as everyone is not "I".

By following such ready-made patterns, we listen to our inner voice less and less and some reach the point where they do not know or no longer know what to do with their lives. That voice that can guide us, we hide it under the cloud of baggage that we gathered at first out of ignorance, then out of the desire not to disappoint or not to be isolated from the many. Unconsciously we are afraid, we are ashamed, we feel complex, we feel worthless. We live with the belief that our words would not have any importance for others, without knowing that these patterns do not define us. All these expressions of fear, and what arises from them, are the basis of an ignorant and easily manipulated existence. In these conditions, the beautiful, good, positive things remain, as Laurent Gounelle says, seeds that instead of cultivating, or entrusting them to the wind, rain and earth, we let them dry in the bottom of our pockets (19).

We learn from family, learn at school, and learn our entire lives. It's just that learning and looking for reason in everything, belongs to our mind, thoughts, belongs to our left hemisphere. The right side is the seat of our intuition and creativity. It is what defines our authenticity and individuality in our expression as beings and as creators. It is what has been sought to be suppressed by those who have knowledge of the ancient teachings and control humanity through fear. They know that a desire is anchored in us through emotions. An image, a thing, a message that incites us produces emotion and the more are created from the outside, just for the sake of following the patterns, the less those inside us, born of our nature, take place. However, the search outside will be in vain, because we will not find what we want, but only what we are, a bundle of fears.

Fear

Nobody likes the existence of fear because we don't like the state it gives us. But the mere idea of getting rid of it means that we unconsciously accept that it exists within us. The reason for doing it is because fear has the most negative influence. According to W. W. Atkinson (38), fear has the most detrimental impact as it poisons the body's cells and leads to the weakest mental state.

Fear, that is considered the lowest emotion, arises from a false sense of unworthiness. This feeling is deemed false because every individual is born with inherent value. However, this sense of lack is instilled during childhood as a result of unprocessed traumas. Our bodies absorb these emotional shocks and store them in the subconscious mind. As children, we could not comprehend what was happening, and those around us at the time were unaware of how to address the situation. They did not realise the necessity of providing the love and support that the child desperately required, which many of us lacked in our society.

The societal system we are born into leads us to believe that our value lies outside of ourselves: in money, societal roles, and material possessions. It is challenging, but it is not impossible to delve deep within oneself and recognise that we have been conditioned by societal norms. Only you hold the power to change your thought patterns, alter your self-perception, and perceive the world from a different perspective. You have the ability to embrace your own duality and see that good and bad are not entirely separate entities, but rather two poles of the same spectrum, thereby accepting both the ego and the higher self.

Of course, there is also the option of "living with your fears." All you have to do is "forget them". When I first read that statement, I smiled. How can I forget them? Forgetting doesn't make them disappear. I can't erase them from my mind and pretend they don't exist because they are deeply embedded in my subconscious. Forgetting them means keeping them and suppressing them even more, like stuffing dirty clothes in a laundry basket. It means accumulating more fears inside me and continuing to live with a baggage I don't want.

The above lines, at which I was smiling, are born from the conviction and righteousness of the author, but each person has their own sense of justice because they possess their own truth. Each of us has our own fears, and the decision to live with them or address them is ours. And to choose the path of fear? Fear is humanity's greatest enemy. Dominique Webb (10) defines it as the obstacle that stands in the way of progress and success. At the same time, it is the tool of leaders in being able to control and manipulate the masses. This is because, as I mentioned before, fear is a negative energy emotion and has the lowest vibrational frequency. Since we are all energy in motion, energies attract energies of the same vibrational frequency. Fear will attract more fear. That's why the things we fear often become reality. Are we afraid of illness? Are we afraid of losing our jobs or running out of money? These fears may come true because we might attract the conditions and events to make them come true, and social media is full of events that only perpetuate fear. To change something, we need to change ourselves, to leave this world of fear we so easily enter as children.

I also briefly explored fear in my previous book (45), but what is the connection between selfishness and fear?

The fears we harbour within us often drive our decisions in life, leading to regrets. I have personally experienced living with anxiety and agitation, worrying about the consequences of my words and actions my mind was creating. There were nights when I struggled and cried, and could not sleep consumed by thoughts of how my words and actions would be interpreted by others and the potential outcomes.

In moments like these, we question what to do, how to do it, when, where, with whom, and why, and we seek answers. Our minds provide responses based on our subconscious, offering endless variations that we meticulously examine to determine the best course of action. Then we twist and turn them in all sorts of ways to see which version is best for the situation in which we find ourselves. Every situation leads to more, creating a track record of options. We wait for confirmation from somewhere, to decide which option is the best for us, to decide the best way forward. However, until these fears are resolved, our selfishness responds using the weapons that our fears put at our disposal.

Based on my experiences, I can say that the more we suppress our fears, the more power they hold over us. They not only attract events that fuel them, and make them grow. They also create mental obstacles that hinder us from achieving our dreams and the limits they impose on you in taking action for what you want.

However, fears are invented by our minds, based on experienced traumas. To what we have inherited ancestrally, we add personal experiences and traumas, that have left their mark on us. These experiences are as I said in the previous chapter, accumulated in childhood and amplified as adults. Those fears are the inner baggage of you, of me, of every human being, baggage that grows throughout life and that we carry wherever we go in this world. They will always question us in everything we do. They will show one-way roads or mazes where you will feel lost. They will grow throughout life being amplified by everything we attract on the same vibrational frequency, and our behaviour will mirror these fears. They keep adding layers, and are "helped" to be maintained or increased, by the mass media, politics and religion. The whole bundle of fears that govern our lives, in short, represents selfishness.

To stay in that vibration of fears, we give them strength through the vocabulary intended for them: "if you do this, it will be...", "if you do differently, it will be..." (it will be different, naturally!) expressions that will guide us in everything that life throws our way. If

there were, then I would... If I had, then I would... If and then....
Known or not to you, the reader, but to me, they are expressions I have
used for many years. Thus, while my mind was searching for the best
ways for an "if", I let precious moments pass me by. Instead of trusting
what I felt, I asked myself countless questions, because as I said in
"The Recipe for Happiness" I lived with anxiety for many years and
learned to endure it (45). I was afraid of mistakes, afraid of failure, of
punishment, I compared myself with others, or compared what I had
with what others had. I was always living a past that had left its traces
inside me, or to paraphrase Carlos Castaneda (6), I let the torch of
anger and humiliation burn inside me for years. All this time, the
present was slipping past me, because living emotionally fuelled by
unresolved traumas, I was actually only living in the past, aiming for
the future.

The past stored in us makes us live with anxiety, agitation,
and nervousness. We expect confirmation from others that what we say
or do is "correct". We have become addicted to "likes" and are looking
for explanations for dislikes. We seek to somehow prove our
superiority. If we don't have the desired confirmation, it seems to us
that we are left out. It's just that all of this is born out of fears that we
are not good, that we are not valuable. And yet, the value is not given
to us by the mistakes or the number of failures and not even by the
likes of the friends that appear like mushrooms after the rain, when
you are "someone". Our value was and always remains within us
because we were born with it. We don't see it or allow ourselves to feel
it because it is suffocated by our fears that become our inner baggage.
I say suffocated because literally, I lived for years feeling like I was
choking on things that I didn't say or do for various reasons just
because they were born out of fear.

*Panic attacks, shaking, sweating, and restlessness, are signs that the body gives us that something is wrong inside us and we look for the blame for our failures, pains and experiences on the outside. These negative experiences, which we call fear, hatred, malice and more, leave their mark on our organs because as W. W. Atkinson (37) also says, **those who have poor health have a gloomy mental state.** It is impossible to be full of worry or anger and remain healthy. Fear, he also says, first strikes the stomach, affecting the blood from there and then, every cell of the body. He also explains that the person suffering from constipation needs to take measures to resolve thoughts born of fear, hatred, anger, and worry.*

By continuing to let that emotional baggage inside us because we know it's a safe place, not knowing or wanting to explore it, accept it and lighten its weight, we're hurting ourselves first and foremost. Looking for options to get rid of it, you won't know which option is best for you until you try it. Even if others have done what you want to do, it does not mean that you too are condemned to the result obtained by them. We each have other experiences, other feelings, and other ways of seeing the world around us because we are unique and then our way of thinking and acting is unique. It's just that no one can take action for us. We are the only ones who can fight for ourselves and our self-esteem, to rediscover our own worth that never disappeared, anywhere, but was buried under our fears.

When we regain it, we dare to be who we feel we want to be. Fears no longer have power over us, the opinions of others no longer affect us. We don't feel the need to have anyone's confirmation. We follow our path without asking ourselves "if". Therefore, we follow the wisdom of our soul that brings us closer to what we need to become in this life, better and more loving people. Eventually, maybe it asks "Why not? What if"?

*I don't know if you, dear reader, have suffered, but I have often regretted decisions made using reason, that is, what seems right to the mind, as Carlos Castaneda says (6). Everything that happened afterwards always proved to me that the intuition, I had not followed, was right. Even though what I was experiencing was accompanied by pain, it was not afraid. The mind is afraid. It always has doubts, seeks and finds infinite ways to surrender to the conditioning of society, thanks to the emotions that are the basis of the filtering of thoughts. Instead, the heart knows no fear. After all, it is connected to love, to intuition because, as David Icke says (9), **it is the bridge to the cosmos.***

The conditioning we are taught to live with makes it difficult, and for many, it seems impossible to live differently. The journey of life is not always smooth; it is filled with trials and failures, and sometimes the truth can be painful. However, the heart knows that everything is for our good. The mind may say "no" or "it's impossible," refusing to accept information that doesn't align with the beliefs stored in our subconscious. By listening to the heart, we will realize that certain information resonates with our truth and should not be rejected. Love simply follows what it knows without limits or conditions, accepting everything as it comes.

The human mind has its role but from my own experience, I can say that when you surrender to it completely, you give power to selfishness, and you close your heart, and the soul suffocates under the baggage of fears and frustrations. You can control the mind, but not the heart and the love you were born from. Romantically speaking, you will not love when and whom you want or when others force you. Love just... is, and when you love, everything seems to be perfect in our world. Nothing seems to bother us and nothing seems to be bad. Again, romantically speaking, each of us has loved at least once in our life. In those moments we know that the world seems more beautiful to us, more different than we knew it. Everything has a different colour, a different scent, and we feel more alive. It is not for nothing that we are told that we are brighter and more beautiful when we love and that happiness can be read on our faces.

When we don't know our worth, we don't know that love is inside us all the time and we look for it outside of us. A search based on a false lack of worth is only a step toward insecurity and low or zero self-esteem. Anyway, that's the purpose of fears and selfishness, to keep you locked up, at their mercy, and you remain just a pawn on the stage of life. It's up to you whether you become their puppet or not. Only you can decide whether to follow your soul or not.

In addition, our unreleased negative emotions tend to grow and accumulate, eventually manifesting as frustration. This buildup can lead to outbursts of anger, ranging from "simple fireworks" to violence, and can be directed at ourselves or others. Often, we don't fully comprehend the source of this intense anger within us. These suppressed emotions can add extra weight, leading us to seek release through means like exercise, diet, or religion. However, the emotions persist, and we may be surprised to find ourselves regaining lost weight or experiencing declining health. Emotions demand to be vented. If they are not expressed, they will manifest as physical ailments. Their explosion in our body takes the form of diseases, or as Lise Bourbeau (20) says, leads to the explosion of our body's cells, and cancer becomes the final expression of unresolved emotions.

The mind is looking for answers to the question "Why did I get sick?", but the source is within us, in our emotions. Stored and suppressed, they also increase our selfishness, that always wants to be in control, but it is only euphoria that goes out at the first stronger storm that hits it.

Maybe you know people who have nowhere near what you have and they are better off and happier than you. Those people understood that our life goes by repeatedly living the past or scrutinising a "future" that we don't know when it comes, only feeding our minds with illusions, born of fear and hope. A boundless future, which may be tomorrow, the day after tomorrow, or never, while the present is here and now. We bypass it when we relive the past or rush to the future. Those people have discovered that their own power is within them and that they can live without fear, because as W. W. Atkinson states, "There is no Devil but Fear - nothing but Fear can hold you back from to one's own inheritance and birthright."(38)

Selfishness

In a "civilised" society where the ego is in power, the selfish one is often considered stronger and more valuable than others. Okakura Kakuzo paints a perfect picture of our selfishness. "We are bad because we are terribly self-aware. We create problems of conscience because we are afraid to tell the truth to others; we take refuge in pride because we are afraid to tell ourselves the truth. How can anyone be serious about the world when the world itself is such a ridiculous thing!" (29)

By understanding your own ego, which you grew up with and have nourished throughout your life, you can see that the false power of those who think they are strong and worthy comes from pure selfishness and a lack of conscious self-worth. With their trust in the external world - in money, castles, weapons, and armies - they do not love themselves and thus are unable to love others. They are too selfish to see beyond the material possessions or social ranks behind which they hide. From the power they have claimed for themselves, they have created patterns in which many people live. However, they know that those who reclaim their inner strength cannot be defeated. They radiate light and love, and they lack even the fear of death because they understand and believe that death is merely a transformation we all experience. Ultimately, the world as viewed through the "subatomic world of the physicists" or the "phenomenological world of the mystical philosopher from the East" is also "a world of continuous birth and death," as Fritoj Kapra states (12).

However, the many who live in fear of tomorrow, fear of death and "divine" punishments are very easy to control and manipulate, which is why W. W. Atkinson (38) compares them to a herd of human sheep who easily follow a leader everywhere, jumping through the same place, even if there are other options. They prefer to copy what others do becoming just servile imitators because it's easier.

They don't realize, and some don't even want to, that they are easily controlled due to their inner fears. They continue to live according to societal patterns, striving for a high position on the hierarchical scale by any means, hoping it will bring them well-being. In this pursuit, they sacrifice their present lives in a never-ending cycle of pain that affects their spirit and emotional well-being, leading to the destruction of their inner balance. Yet, they often chase illusions throughout their lives and die filled with regrets.

However, can you find the peace and happiness you long for in a society filled with fear, hypocrisy, malice, and violence? Can you find the strength to remove that evil and pain that gnaws you internally? **It depends only on you…**

Selfishness is always hungry for power, and wealth, constantly seeking something new to devour. It's like a bottomless bucket you struggle to fill; the more you do, the less you see collected in it. The more selfish you become, the further you are from the source of all that exists, from love, turning desperately to violence and acts of self-destruction.

From a young age, we are taught to value labels and the power of money, fostering selfishness and respect for the "big and strong". Filled with fears, we grow and cling to them hoping that the solutions our minds offer will help us escape their prison. However, all the defense we build is false and falls with every new life lesson life teaches us. Every weapon that fears use to defend their existence falls, and disintegrates. There are ways in which the universe keeps showing us that we are not on the right path and we need to change it or, as W. W. Atkinson (37) states, to change the mental attitude.

Our genetic material as humans is a transmitter-receiver of frequencies says David Icke (9). Love resonates with a high vibrational frequency on a short wavelength, while the emotion of fear resonates with a very low vibrational frequency on a long wavelength, as the opposite of love. If each wave of energy represents another, totally different universe, change, as Carlos Castaneda (6) expresses, means only movement in the bands of energy fields perceived as our everyday life.

To return to the frequency of love, we need to change the frequency of fear, which involves connecting with our subconscious. This process is comparable to Carlos Castaneda's idea of "returning to the spirit after descending into hell. And from hell we bring trophies. One of those is understanding." (6)

As I have already said, the family of selfishness is very numerous and leads us in every area of our life. Very often we don't even know how selfish we are, because we act and react out of habit.

Just because I've been down this road and understand it doesn't mean I expect you to agree with me. However, you may recognize selfishness if:

• *You always want to be right, as the ego has a hard time believing and most of the time it doesn't believe that we too are wrong or could make mistakes. It associates mistakes with weakness and foolishness.*

• *You want to prove your righteousness and you seek to do it by any means;*

• *You consider yourself a victim, either of other people or of the events that happened around you;*

• *You look for blame in others and things outside of you.*

• *You don't accept that you are selfish or doing it limited;*

• *You are always comparing yourself to others in the way you look, in your work, in everything you have.*

• *Whatever you will have and do, you will have a continuous anger-governed dissatisfaction inside you.*

• *You give up on many dreams because you think you don't have what it takes to achieve them and thus live the life you want.*

• *You direct your hatred towards others, when in fact you unconsciously hate yourself.*

• *You look for the faults of others in order to feel better than them;*

• *You don't like change because you feel like you are losing the comfort you know. However, everything is constantly changing. It is evolving. Nothing stands still.*

• *You prefer not to have responsibilities or to get rid of them quickly.*

• *You want to have more responsibilities than others, to prove to yourself and others you are worthy, and to feel proud.*

• *You envy others for everything they have or live, while you are a victim of fate and society.*

Thus, among others, victimhood, arrogance, cowardice, greed, hatred, and revenge are part of the family of selfishness and it uses these to prove to you the reasons behind the thoughts you have or actions you take. But all these motives, the mechanisms under which they act, are fakes. The base from which it operates is built on falsehood, on a mountain of fears. It is enough to start removing just one and the "power" of the ego is shaken, the foundation begins to shake, and its "power" falls like a castle of cards.

This mountain of fear is used to the full to control our thoughts, emotions and actions. At the same time, the bigger your ego, the more you unconsciously hate yourself. I know it seems hard to believe, but as I said before, everything I write comes from my own experiences, and from the lessons my life has given me.

What does the ego dislike? In the pursuit of false perfection, the ego uses fears to divert our attention from remembering who we are and what our life goals are as Doreen Virtue says (11). It dislikes its fears, but it is built and grows up using them for its own benefit, seeking to prove that it is the best at everything.

Any difference it sees between you and others, it uses to prove in one way or another that you are better than another or even the best. At the same time, it uses differences to have what it considers to be power over others. Feeling humiliated or weak, it gives strength to arrogance, pride, cowardice, greed...

It dislikes mistakes because it feels weak, meaning that it loses its strength. It doesn't like to be wrong, even if, consciously, deep inside, the person knows it shouldn't be doing what it's doing. But selfishness does not accept it. That plays cat and mouse with you in the quest to dominate and possess everything it wants, in any form and from any point of view. It will look for reasons to prove its righteousness, and it does it by appealing to all its virtues. It will use pride, violence, weakness, revenge, victimization...

In some cases, it even despises compassion. As a victim, a selfish man seeks others' sympathy, for himself. If irony and the feeling of being considered weak or worthless shines through, it turns again to pride, revenge, violence.

It also dislikes reproaches as it touches its sensitivity, making it feel the existence of weakness, imperfection and worthlessness. It feels humiliated, and for our lower self it means increasing arrogance or leads to anxiety and depression.

Despite being negative traits, many of us observe these in others but find it challenging to accept them in ourselves. However, the flaws we see in others also exist within us. Everything you see wrong on the outside is inside you waiting to be found and resolved. Selfishness prevents us from recognizing these traits within ourselves, as acknowledging them would mean putting him aside, and out of a desire to rule, it wants you to be its slave.

By delving deep within, we can truly understand ourselves and see instances of our own selfishness, often without realizing it. Only by exploring the darkness of your lower self you accept the existence of fears and stored trauma. It is the path where we uncover and confront those fears and past traumas, a process that is challenging, but not impossible. Furthermore, the deeper and deeper you delve and the more fears you find, the greater the darkness you will enter. That abyss that you will feel to the full, brings pain and... other fears to light.

Why do we have so many fears? Our past experiences hold the origins of our traumas. We are born with unresolved emotional patterns and passed down from generation to generation to which all the others that come from our traumas will be added. The older and deeper the fear, the stronger it becomes. In addition, it will not act for your benefit, but only to your detriment.

Being trained to follow other people's ideas, we conform to other people's demands and it seems normal to live in this way. Moreover, most of what we are allowed to know or are given "on a plate" is negative news that only feeds these fears we already have. We are given matrices to sit comfortably in without allowing us to truly know ourselves. We don't know, we don't want to, we can't live otherwise because we are afraid. We have been taught to trample on our own opinions, ideas, and dreams just because they don't agree with the ideas of others who we see as better or worthier than us, and we do it because that's the only way we can comply with the norms imposed by society. Even if we don't like much or anything in what we do, we follow their path just to do what they dictate, as we hope for happiness, but our actions are based on selfishness. Thus, we come to want more and more, but not in the sense of evolution, but in the sense of accumulation, and at some point we find that we are still unhappy. We seek confirmation of worth and self-esteem through whatever we can find on the outside.

Our search will be rewarded with lessons, because "life is a succession of lessons that must be lived to be understood" says Ralph Waldo Emerson. The most important lessons are the ones that hurt the most, and something that hurts selfishness so damn bad is what we call failure. However, failures are experiences that help us discover ourselves. They guide us in discovering not only our fears but also the power we have to begin changing ourselves and changing our lives. By opening our minds, we can descend into our souls to explore our pain, discover our fears and accept them. Do you think it is not possible? From my own experience, I can say that it is possible because they are also part of us. This is the only way we manage to open the doors of the soul, freeing it from the baggage that we have thrown onto its shoulders in the past and carried after us for many years. By accepting them, we accept ourselves exactly as our soul tells us to be.

Without getting out of the prison of fear and demolishing selfishness, it suffocates the relationships we live not only with those who are "strangers" to each other but also within the family. In couples, the woman wants to control all the actions of the man. It doesn't mean that there isn't the other option, especially if we think about man's pride. But in these couples, true love does not speak. In them, each person's selfishness speaks in his language, and both live from their fears that fuel their jealousy, thirst for control and manipulation of their partner. He does not want to be deceived but asserts the right to do so. She seeks satisfaction in the bed of another but wants proof of love from her partner. We claim that we live in a more evolved society, but now, as in the past, women look for the same things in men, resources and good hunting qualities, and men look for everything that their ancestors also looked for in women: physical beauty and health. However, accepting anything from your partner or doing anything only to maintain a relationship builds up anger and resentment and they will attract emotional abuse. We need to look for people who want to be with us, not need us, as Allan Pease says (3).

Although problem-free relationships are only found in movies and children's stories, there are some couples with similar values and beliefs about life (3). Leaving aside the couples who prefer to live comfortably ignoring each other, some couples stand the test of time because they manage to find a balance in the life they have built together through everything they have experienced along the way. They have found the ability to deal with the differences of opinion that arise in the relationship and to seek and apply mutual understanding and fulfilment of the partner's needs, a condition of happiness in a relationship.

Similar understanding and fulfilment of needs are necessary in parent-child relationships as well. Yet, the most challenging relationships occur between authoritarian parents and their children. These parents who, in turn, have not known true love because they did not experience it as children, will become manipulators and controllers of their own children's lives, going as far as to demand blind obedience. My childhood is one such example, and acknowledging what I experienced does not mean that I condemn my parents or that I do not love them. Because of these relationships, I had to fight my own internal battle to understand that the way I was raised was the only way they knew it. It wasn't their fault and it wasn't mine either. Even though I suffered, cried and had to "fight" with the ideas that were imposed on me under the slogan of the norms of "must" that reflect the patterns of society, I am grateful for everything I have experienced. They were the ones who assumed the role of being my parents and guided me to reach the path I am on today.

As a parent myself, I tried to do the same with my own child. In addition, on the one hand, as a single mother I tried to fulfil the role of the father, and those who are single mothers know what I'm talking about. On the other hand, being "addicted" to studies, and striving for perfection, I also tried to guide my child to follow a similar path. Except that one day, when the child, who was not yet a teenager, told me that he would not follow the path I suggested, because he would have to "hit the upper threshold to see the lower one". Although his words left me speechless, I slowly began to understand how selfish I was in my motherly love. He made me think that due to my past, in which I had not been freed from emotional obstacles, from fears, I was trying to make my child follow a path that mirrored my own, rather than allowing him to find his own way. His words brought me in front of his truth as a child and as a future adult. They put me in front of my own truth which is not very easy to digest. I was reacting unconsciously and destructively, because as Alice Miller says in The Awakening of Eve (1), I was trying to survive the traumas and their consequences, still being a slave to them and their hidden emotions.

By recognizing the behaviour patterns of our parents in ourselves, we no longer blindly repeat them in turn with our own children. Even if we were not brought up by methods based on fear and punishment, as adults it is difficult for us to give justice to a child, a being smaller than us, and the confrontation with our own child brings us in front of emotions that we do not think we have in us, which is why it is difficult for us to accept them.

You may be familiar with the expressions "shut up, you're a child," "shut up, you're small," and "you have to listen to adults." There was a time when I also agreed with this type of thinking.

An incident I experienced a few years ago confirmed to me again how strongly selfishness believes in the "biggest" and ignores the "small." In a discussion with several teenagers and adults, one of the adults stated in a loud and blunt voice that a child should shut up and listen to their elders. I told the man that every being has the right to express his opinion, and he vehemently retorted, "do you say that I, an old man, must listen to a child?" I replied, "You don't have to, but if you want, you can at least listen to him, because even adults can learn from children."

It may be hard for us to admit, but sometimes a child brings to the surface fears adults refuse to see or don't even know they have. If we accept to shed the ego shell, we will understand that age is just a number and is not a proof of wisdom. People who have been dead perhaps for a very long time remain alive in the memory of posterity because of their mind and character, because of the legacy they left in people's souls, and not because of their longevity. The wisdom of the soul knows no age.

Many times our reactions as adults and parents, even though we reason them to be for the good of our child, will not do good to him. Thus, our first tendency when a child speaks his mind is to tell him to shut up. He is ignored, pushed aside or given "rewards" for not bothering. Our reaction will leave its mark on that child, and the consequences will be seen in time, in the way he will react to the relationships he will build and to everything that life will offer him. Thus, from anxious parents, children will be born with even greater emotional problems. They will become worse during his life due to his own negative experiences. What will their children be like? I'll let you answer for yourself.

We think we know our children so well that we know what they want. Many times, "out of too much love" we limit them and chip away at their self-confidence. From our false lack of value that we have lived or still live with, we project our dreams onto our children to make them come true. We indeed know them because we have seen them grow up before our eyes, but we do not live in their inner world to understand their feelings and how deep they are. Even though he is your child, he is a unique being, as every human is, and this means that his emotions may be on a completely different level than mine as a parent. They will be able to be stronger or not, to be able to express them or not. Our child is another human being and we did not bring him into this world to control or manipulate him in the direction we wanted. He needs support and a lot of love, but not the conditional love, because he doesn't need a selfish love. Instead of being criticised, he needs to be helped to develop, and mature. He needs pure love that will teach him and help him to build respect for his being and his dreams and needs us to support him in the path of life no matter what it is. This support does not mean money, clothes or gadgets. It means helping him see the bright side of mistakes, to understand and learn from them. It means that he sees you are not ashamed because you do not know everything, and that you also make mistakes; he needs to see that you admit your mistakes and ask for forgiveness or that you know how to say thank you. As parents we are there for them physically, but do we do it emotionally? Or how often do we do it?

The education we give the child promoted through our traumas, will lead to the child's lack of self-esteem, making him just another anonymous or emotionally immature pawn in the great mass. Another depersonalized member, following the patterns of society, without knowing himself, his abilities and his limits. To help him become himself, we can choose to see him as Kahlil Gibran presents him:

> *"Your children are not your children.*
> *They are the sons and daughters of Life's*
> *longing for it*
> *itself.*
> *They come through you but not from you,*
> *And although they are with you, they are not yours.*
> *You can give them love,*
> *but they are not your thoughts,*
> *Because they have their thoughts.*
> *You can accommodate their body but not their soul..." (17)*

Out of sincere love, you don't force the child to become your copy, to do what you want, to follow the path you set it. Nor are you asking him to trample his own dreams and desires and his own self with them. You pay attention to his privacy, his vital space, you don't try to direct his life as you want just because "that's the way it should be", "that's the best way", "that's how you'll live better", "you don't know how the world works". You don't project your own dreams onto the child to live them through him. Don't build illusory happiness on your own child's unhappiness!

True love means forgiveness and accepting mistakes as lessons. It involves support, encouragement, respect, and taking responsibility for one's actions. It also means understanding that everyone has the right to follow their own path as they see it. In a relationship or family, true love gives you the power to communicate honestly with your partner, communication that is the cornerstone of trust. It involves expressing one's feelings and desires without fear of anger or arguments, without fear of consequences. In the relationship between parents and children, it means avoiding phrases like "I am the parent and you are the child", "I know what's best because I am your parent, not you mine".

However, to truly know and experience what is called unconditional love requires acceptance of one's selfishness and forgiveness. You need to know your inner self to make room for love. Like it or not, suffering is a natural part of our inner healing process. People I've worked with to resolve their emotions have told me "I don't want to suffer" or "I've suffered enough, I don't want any more suffering". Just like how a wound hurts before it heals, experiencing pain is a vital step in the healing process. It's like getting pricked by thorns when tending to a rose garden. The same with our experiences. You need to bring them to the surface. Even with outside help to guide you, you need to understand that you will experience pain, that you will suffer and cry, and that you will have to deal with it alone because no one, even if they wanted to, can relive the trauma for you. Dealing with emotional pain is a personal journey. After releasing emotions, you will feel lighter, having the feeling that something has left you. We are used to saying that "it's like a stone has been removed from my heart", "it's like I got rid of a boulder from behind", "I feel lighter". Frankly speaking, it is. We express what is happening. We feel their release from the prison of fear.

Although these fears misguide our thoughts and emotions, they are what bring us the storms of life. Without them we would find no direction on the path of life. They are part of the salt and pepper of our life and we need to learn from them for our personal growth. When they bring you down, no one can force you up. Just as the eagle uses the storm to soar higher, you are the only one who can truly help yourself, because no one can do it for you. No one outside of you will know, feel or be capable of what you are capable of, because no one can live your life. No one will give you the value you don't give yourself. How you use the storms in your life is up to you. It's your choice to stay on your knees or rise higher than you were. No one can help you if you don't help yourself.

You can't control anything outside of your thoughts and emotions. Instead, with the understanding that you can't change anyone or anything outside of you, you can find the balance you long for. By releasing your negative emotions, you can come to understand that the outcomes of the situations driven by selfishness will have a different ending through the changes you make.

In fact, beyond the harm that selfishness causes in our world - dividing us as humanity, nations, or tearing apart our families - it can also help us understand that without it, and without the darkness it has cast upon us as humanity, we cannot appreciate the magnitude of the desire to find and use the light.

Failure

One of the obstacles the mind puts up for us comes from failure. For years, any failure meant guilt for me. It made me feel like I hadn't learned enough, or that I wasn't good enough. I used to attribute any failure to myself, or sometimes to others around me. In our society, any failure is punished in different forms, which prevents us from making more mistakes. That's because I didn't have the knowledge that encountering obstacles, I was looking for solutions and learning to overcome them, and in this way, I was learning to move on.

From the pattern of failure and its repercussions, I used to believe that making a mistake was not allowed and it was something bad. As many others, I saw a mistake as the end of something, without understanding that every end means a new beginning. I didn't know that fear was my teacher. Out of fear, we often don't continue what we have done before, or try again, or try something new. Fear of the unknown, fear of pain, fear of failure, just... fear.

By putting the failure under the microscope, I was also saying in "The Recipe for Happiness" (45) that there was something I didn't know because I didn't have the necessary knowledge at that time. Every failure presents an opportunity for a new beginning, and changing something in the way we approach can lead to positive change for us.

We don't like changes, but they are a sign of our evolution and the recovery of self-esteem. Knowing that you are born worthy, failure is no longer an obstacle, but a blessing that teaches you to move forward without fear.

3. Army of Fears

There is nothing to be afraid of except Fear—so the sooner you cast off Fear the better you will be, and the more advanced on the road to Mastery.

W. W. Atkinson (38)

We all need love, and even more so a child. Receiving it, especially at an age when he cannot call upon the knowledge of the mind and the understanding of emotions, will alleviate the negative experience or even make it dissipate. Because of the love that was not given to us, we will not know that true love until we decide that we need to look in our past for what brought pain and suffering. To free our intuition from the yoke of fear, we may need to make changes in our lives.

Perhaps you are familiar with the unease that someone's words, discussion, or actions bring to you. You feel agitated and nervous because you think there will be consequences and you don't know them, you don't know how you will react because you don't know how they will affect you. All these experiences are brought to the surface by the fear of not being able to face what might happen to you, that you can't handle it, that it won't be good or... that you will die. We are afraid of fear, and the false worthlessness it supports will manifest itself in different forms and be experienced differently by each person. What they will have in common will be restlessness, anxiety, the desire to please others, to give up their own ideas, dreams, and desires, or to use the weapons of fear to build a wall of defence. We will resort to them while we live in the world of selfishness, to counteract these states that we dislike, because we do not want to feel them.

Procrastination

One of the first weapons of fear, which we begin to use, is procrastination, because, in a way, it is the first one that is offered to us as children.

This behaviour is often learned in childhood from the moment of love that we reach for a moment of attention, a moment that is always put on hold: "I can't now", "you see, I'm busy", "later", by adults. As children, we interpret this as a rejection, feeling unimportant and unworthy of adult attention. The child feels he is not as important as others or as certain things that keep his parent away from him when he demands attention. Unconsciously, he takes it that he is being rejected because he is not worth enough to be given the adult's attention.

By using procrastination as adults, we trample on our self-confidence, which is already chipped away by what we experienced as children. It becomes a "weapon" we use we punish ourselves or try to punish others.

To understand it from the point of view of selfishness, we dismiss the procrastinations that we have in life for reasons that are not directly dependent on us. Although, being attracted by our thoughts, they also happen in our life for a reason. Going back to procrastination, it is the one we give ourselves as a punishment because we don't know where to begin to approach a situation, an event, or we don't know how to continue it. Theoretically, we know that anything new requires more or less time to be known and understood, but living with a bundle of fears inside us, we very often resort to postponing everything possible, some all our lives. We put off answers or put off actions. The mind knows that we are not good enough and we will live with the idea that we will not achieve what we have to do and prefer to resort to procrastination. As a false form of forgiving ourselves, the mind will look for and give us reasons not to take certain actions, and nowadays the most frequently used reasons are "I don't have time" and "I don't have money".

Do we really not have time? Time measured in whatever unit of measure we want, just follows its course. It is the same or to put it another way, the day is always 24 hours as we are taught to measure it. Sometimes, in our selfishness, we also want time to be measured differently than we know, only that regardless of the demand of our mind, time just is. We measure it and evaluate ourselves based on what we do or don't do in this measured time, and we are the ones who let it pass us by. We are the ones who live our lives or behave like the "living dead".

I recently heard a line from a movie that really resonated with me: "You live to make money. I live to make time. That is my wealth." This quote reflects the reality of our world. We often prioritize making money over making time for ourselves and the things we truly enjoy. In fact, the continuous running to workplaces, schools, shops, for daily problems, to acquire more money for more things outside of us, "has put our senses to sleep" as Carlos Castaneda says (6). As a result, we chase after material possessions and external sources of happiness, neglecting our inner selves and intuition.

I understand the importance of money in our society. However, the money we work for is collected by others to pay taxes (on OUR work), TV, houses and cars bought from OUR work, using OUR health, etc. Money "took away not only our eyes" offering us false confidence and freedom, but as the Romanian saying goes, "it also took away our minds". Money conditions you when, where, how to live and work, when, where and with whom to feel good, when, where and what to have to be okay with yourself, although prosperity, as Clive Staples Lewis says (7) makes man think that he has found his place in the world, that he is at home here among earthly things, but the reality is that the world has found its place in him. Money itself is only a shilling of false value and gives conditional freedom. If you were to strip many of the very rich, of all the wealth they have accumulated, you would see that they are nothing more than selfish people, full of fears they have no idea or don't want to know. On the other hand, mountains of money you will have, you will never be okay, if inside you are not good with yourself, if you have not reached your own inner harmony.

Procrastination, as I said, exists because of our false lack of value. We often procrastinate out of fear of making mistakes, being punished, or the daunting nature of the task.

It is also handy when what we have to do seems too complicated because, in our selfish society, everything has to be done as fast as possible and in large quantity, even if the results are of poor quality. Everything is expected to generate value, which is typically equated with money. Thus, to get rid of these chores, egoism resorts to all kinds of feel-good strategies. Therefore, to avoid these responsibilities, people often resort to activities that provide instant gratification, such as watching TV, drinking excessively, gossiping, or engaging in activities that require minimal effort (e.g. eating seeds of boredom). Some people prefer to cry and complain about others, but they "sit and wait" for something better to come into their lives as a gift. That means doing anything else that doesn't require effort or stepping out of your comfort zone. Something that the mind finds very easy because procrastination is a false way of escaping the mind from the straps in which it feels corseted by fears.

Being honest with ourselves we will see how many times we have postponed our actions in life or left them unfinished for various reasons. Some of them may have been resumed and finished, others have remained and will remain suspended in the ether for a long time or perhaps for a lifetime. Going down inside you will find yourself full of frustrations, you will find blame and spite, all born from such procrastination, and they will look for external victims, only among them, we will be the first victims.

We postpone answers desired by others, answers demanded by our children, and we postpone everything that can be postponed, *but procrastination reflects a lack of self-trust and self-worth, as well as a lack of trust in others, that comes from the same lack of worth we live with, without knowing that we have it.*

When we don't need procrastination or are aware of the reasons why we resort to it, we are being honest with ourselves. When not, we end up switching weapons and resorting to repression.

Repression

Many of us were indirectly or directly forbidden from expressing or acting on our emotions as children. As a result, we suppressed them. If any other repressed emotion appears, it adds to the existing one, making the energy ball of emotion grow over time. When left unresolved but constantly fed, it can lead to the formation of a cyst or tumour in medical terms.

Emotions are energy in motion and they need to be expressed. We didn't do it or we don't do it because we have enough "reasons" in the form of the expressions "the world sees you", "the world hears you", "you make me ashamed", and "shame on you". I grew up surrounded by these kinds of expressions and used them myself. It was all those around me and I knew at that time. We were brought up in the corset of some rules imposed by the so-called moral norms and rules.

The question that comes to mind is, "Which world" sees or hears you? Most people are doing the same. Does that world have nothing better to do than to focus on me or you? If they do, it means one of two things: either I/you are the centre of their world, or they're simply bored and don't know what to do with their own lives. However, why should I care about the "mouth of the world"? As long as I follow my intuition, it never guides me to do harm but rather encourages me to follow my own path and live my life authentically.

Whenever we care more about someone else, about other people's opinions, we repress our own emotions, thoughts, and actions. Every repression hurts more and more until you resort to a "false cure" or reach the point where you feel that you need to change something about yourself, to live your life in a different way than you did it before. You will look for ways to escape the pain of these repressions by turning to those "older" than you, to friends, to doctors, and priests. It's just that each of them treats the effects, not the causes, of your pain.

I remember that during the last year when I lived in the flat, I brought water every morning from a nearby spring and on my way I met about the same people every day. Being summer and hot, I used to take a moment to walk barefoot on the grass, basking in the sunshine. I love the contact with the ground and the warmth of the sun. The few passers-by who were there at that time of the morning looked at me circumspectly or ignored me.

One morning, a person who looked older than me (maybe he wasn't, haha, but that's how I saw him) stopped to strike up a conversation. He expressed his scepticism towards doctors, believing they only rely on knowledge passed down from others and couldn't fully understand his own body as he could. "Why should he see me? The doctor only tells me what he has learned from what others have said or written. But, are we the same? I know best what bothers me in my body."

It is the same with our emotions. It's important to remember that you have the deepest insight into your own feelings and what may be causing you inner turmoil. No one else can understand your emotions better than you can, as they do not have access to your soul and the things that trouble you. Seeking guidance from counsellors, mentors, or religious figures is completely fine, but it's essential to see that they will offer advice based on their own experiences, education, or personal interests. The real work of sorting through our internal struggles must be done by each of us individually. No one else can fully comprehend or experience our inner pain in the same way we do. Only you have insight into your own depths. Even those who care deeply for you may be unable to assist if you are not prepared to confront, examine, and come to terms with your past traumas. Taking medication or attending religious services may provide temporary relief, but ultimately, as with anything, the choice is yours.

It's important to understand, and acknowledge our emotions as they exist within us. It's not anyone's fault that these emotions are a part of us. Without delving into the root of our fears, we may try to avoid them, leading to continued pain, or we may confront them and the pain they bring us or we accept... "to burn ourselves".

If you've ever worked in a garden, think of a plant that you want to grow and bear fruit. Even though you know you should weed out the unwanted plants, you might choose to let them grow because it's what most people around you are doing or because you believe it's the best approach. The same goes for your emotions. Whether you choose to ignore them because others are doing so or because you don't believe they matter, it's ultimately up to you. The decision to address your emotions or not is yours to make.

When we suppress our emotions, it's not just about holding them in. It also involves a lack of open communication with both ourselves and others.

Direct communication, where we can interpret body language, facial expressions, and the intensity of someone's gaze, has largely been replaced by technology. As emotional beings, we require direct communication. However, our inability to express our emotions creatively and our tendency to repress them have turned us into puppets. Constantly influenced by external factors to focus on our rational left hemisphere, we have neglected our intuitive, creative, and spiritually connected right hemisphere. Our individuality has been stifled and silenced since childhood, marked as "forbidden" whenever we have tried to act against the wishes of the adults around us. We buried our intuition and creative energy under the weight of logic and the false power of "must", and as the saying goes, "the mind gives birth to monsters," right?

Confirmation

The moment of love we have been deprived of, which comes bundled with the seed of worthlessness, will constantly seek confirmation of the quality of our thoughts and actions. It's just that, often in this selfish society, those who are "ennobled" to offer confirmations of our actions are people driven by much more selfishness than we are.

In the family, the child will seek confirmation from parents, outside the family, from teachers, from friends. His search in life will extend to drugs, alcohol, sex, and for some, the whole life will be a search for confirmation of worth.

The pyramid of power created in our society forced us to live on all levels with the need for confirmations provided by the existence of hierarchy. Even the creation that is born from us is directed to go only in certain directions. Everything that does not respect the rules established by the "centre" or does not find confirmation "from above", "from the big ones", is often disregarded or even destroyed. Consequently, this constant quest for validation can lead to a lack of self-confidence and a false sense of worthlessness. Furthermore, based on our fears, the lack of confirmation causes us disappointment. By adding ridicule, we will suffer even more.

Furthermore, our subconscious mind stores traumas, and one of them that comes through the ancestral line is the one related to "size". Thus, great is the boss, although he may reach up to our chests. Great is the teacher who grades you badly, even though you have learned the lesson. The politician is great because he makes the law. The priest is great because he is the "man of God". Thus, everything that can be defined in one way or another as "big/great", can bring us pain in one way or another, and fear will direct us to seek confirmation from them, often doing or saying what it gives us no pleasure.

We seek appreciation on all levels. It's the reason why we suffer because we don't receive enough likes on social media posts. Our lack of contentment and our happiness becomes dependent on these confirmations and appreciations of value that is falsely small or almost non-existent in us. This leads to anxiety, becoming an obstacle to achieving our goals, because anxiety disturbs our aura and our vibrations become chaotic. (10)

The lack of validation brings pain and suffering, eroding our self-trust and reinforcing feelings of inadequacy and lovelessness. The stronger the anxiety, the more prolonged and intense our state of restlessness becomes, making it feel like the only familiar and comfortable state to exist in.

When we don't receive the expected validation, we compare ourselves to those who do and seek a way to be seen as being worthy, too.

Comparison

The lack of confirmations puts us in the position of comparing ourselves to those who receive them and finding a way to have them too, to be seen as worthy. To put it another way, I use Okakura Kakuzo's (29) question, "Why do people like to advertise themselves so much?" In search of false value, we find ourselves selling out for "a handful of gold", and Okakura Kakuzo astutely observes, "Look at the contented salesman who sells Good and Truth by the piece. One can even buy a Religion, which is nothing but a sanctified morality with flowers and music. Take away the Church's paraphernalia and what is left? Nevertheless, this kind of business thrives wonderfully, because the prices are absurdly low, a prayer for a ticket to heaven, a diploma for a civic honor. Hide as fast as you can, for if your true worth were known to the world, you would quickly be sold to the highest bidder." (29)

The process of evolution implies change and transformation. Our society is constantly changing, yet it has always had needs, resulting in the emergence of moral standards that often sacrifice our individuality on the altar of this "good". As a result, we live in times when the educational system encourages and perpetuates ignorance and intellectual theft. The church offers conditional forgiveness as a ticket to a false heaven, and religion extends love with the condition of becoming a "slave" to it. One gains respect by acting with cowardice and thirsting for false power, whose value is reflected in the glitter of gold and heaps of money.

We choose to live recklessly and arrogantly, hiding the truth about ourselves because we do not want the truth of others to be known. We prefer spite, hatred, envy in order not to reveal our natural vulnerability. We live in a strange world, or as Okakura Kakuzo says, the world has become something ridiculous, and then who will take it seriously? Truth and good are barter for money and false value. (29)

From a young age, we are taught to compare and judge each other, creating a divide between "me" and others. As we grow up, we raise the bar of comparison to higher standards. Thus, to demonstrate the thirst for power that selfishness uses, we steal and make war with each other. It seems that although we call ourselves "civilized", we have not yet learned the lessons that nature knows, respects and offers from times unknown yet. We live our lives running from poverty, seeking an external wealth. We run from ugliness and seek outer beauty. We constantly oscillate between boundaries set by the norms of a superficial society.

We see ourselves as rich or poor, beautiful or ugly, good or bad, and compete for their supremacy. All this comparison brings division and pain, and by running between these limits which we accept as conditions of our existence, we sacrifice the life we have "now".

Who can say what is beautiful and what is ugly? In this difference that defines us, there is no unit of measure, no standard. Being so different it's normal to have our own tastes. Who set the standard of beauty? What one sees as beautiful, another may see as ugly. Our perception and experience is different. The attraction to the beautiful/ugly is due to the energy we emanate ourselves and the resonance we have with the respective persons. Whether we feel ugly or see ourselves as beautiful, that's how others will see us. Everything starts from within us, because as Franklin D. Roosevelt said, "Men are not prisoners of destiny, but only prisoners of their own minds." (44)

Good and bad? All people are good, but the experiences they've had and how they've learned to use them make them act in such a way that they're seen as bad. They are so shaken up inside that the only way they can get their pain out is to make others feel the pain. In their naivety, they think they will feel good doing things that hurt others around them. It is the sum of the experiences they lived fed by hatred, malice, aggression, it is the result of the cruelty of the "black pedagogy" methods Alice Miller talks about (2). And then, could they offer anything else to society than what they have inside, and they don't know their own traumas or how to get rid of their own demons? By judging and condemning them in every way, the rest of us are not helping them. On the contrary, we trample their soul even more, tearing it to pieces, turning them into even greater victims. They don't need to be compared to those who follow or pretend to follow society's norms. They need the touch of love that was perhaps never given to them to come to their own acceptance and forgiveness of what they have experienced to come to accept the way they live.

Beauty exists in every being in so many ways, and everyone's worth and wealth lies within their soul. Do you think that having more money makes you better or more beautiful than others? The idea that having money means having everything is arrogant and selfish. Even if someone buys anything today, neither yesterday, nor today, nor tomorrow will they be able to buy true love. All the gold in the world will never replace your sufferings or fears. They will remain with you until you decide what to do with them. You can seek refuge outside, I know, but you will be met by many masks and standards of false morality.

There is no need to see yourself as better or worse than others! Comparing yourself to others can make you feel insufficiently good or valuable, or excessively valuable. Look in the mirror as many times as you can and see yourself as a being like any other, but at the same time completely different. See yourself worthy, capable of doing good, of loving and being loved. See yourself unique as everyone else is unique in their own way. **Don't compare yourself to anyone because no one is you and you are not no one***!*

Even though we have been taught to believe that we are tall, short, beautiful, ugly, rich, poor, these are just the characteristics of the garment - the body - that we wear in this life. Since souls come from the same source, they use the body as a garment that provides the difference and beauty visible in our material world.

If we can read a book without judging it by its cover, but seek to discover what it hides between its covers, we can seek to appreciate the good and the beautiful in ourselves. Just as every book has a unique message to offer because it has the imprint of the soul value of the one who wrote it, every person is born worthy!

Standardization

Living under repressions, false confirmations, and comparisons because we fail to recognize our inherent value, we easily fall into the trap of accepting and imposing "standardizations" or normalizations. While these are terms often associated with exams and technical aspects, it's not unusual for us to apply them to ourselves and our peers.

In our educated society, we are often afraid of fear itself. Therefore, when we believe we have disappointed someone, we try to rectify the situation by either appealing to our own cowardice or exploiting the weaknesses of the disappointed individual. It's like attempting to make amends for our mistakes because we feel uneasy about what we've done. We fail to acknowledge that the other person's disappointment may stem from their lack of information, attachments, or fears. We strive to make them like us or mould them into our likeness. We seek to think alike, if possible.

What are the reasons behind so many standardizations in the educational system? Why do we attempt to limit children's abilities or categorize everyone into the same "bucket"? Doesn't the beauty of humanity lie in our individuality, authenticity, and originality? What kind of world would we live in if we were all the same height, weight, and colour? Wouldn't it be a dull world?

As long as we fail to see our own individuality, we are unable to respect others', standing between the chains that we build ourselves, as W. W. Atkinson says (38). This lack of appreciation for individuality leads to widespread "copying," large-scale plagiarism, and the prevalence of illiteracy and ignorance in today's technological era. The widespread dissemination of education and scientific knowledge through print, radio, and TV, as pointed out by Dan Farcaş (8), has brought with them not only advantages but, drawbacks, with the latter magnifying over time. When individuals think and behave in uniform ways, they distort reality and avoid what they consider to be "non-essential details." By rejecting individuality, which transcends established patterns, humanity as a whole misses the opportunity to gain new perspectives on problems, situations, and actions. Embracing our uniqueness – without condemnation or a desire for change (5) – as expressed in the proverb "Live as you like and let me live too!" entails showing respect for everyone's individuality, regardless of its nature.

As I reminisce, I find myself transported back decades to my days as an 11th-grade student at the Pedagogical High School, participating in the national phase of a philosophy olympiad. Amidst the emotions, anxiety, and "sweats" I experienced upon seeing the subject written on the blackboard, I was also captivated by the behaviour of one of the supervising teachers. This teacher displayed great care towards a student's work in the room, which caught my attention and set my thoughts in motion. I pondered the nature of genuine competition and contemplated the strategies for winning, all during the time of communism... (Ha, ha!)

After submitting my paper, I told my teacher about the issues I encountered during the Olympiad. He became pale, and with no comments, he informed me that I was chosen, along with other students, for a radio interview.

During the interview, we all were asked to share our thoughts on the Olympics. We had to answer very briefly and if we could have nothing but praise for the contest and the organizers.

My answer was not the expected one, a standard one. I gave my honest opinion, which didn't align with their expectations. The reporter stopped the tape and told me that what I was saying was not very nice and to try to "sweeten" the answer. I can't use the words "unfortunately" but I didn't do what he asked and I stood my ground. He stopped the tape again and again insisted on changing the answer. The third time he didn't stop, but as you can imagine, my "interview" was never broadcast (46). Now, I can understand that there was no way they could do that either because my answer was not within the standard range. It was not up to the requirements and it was perceived as harmful. At that time I was angry at what I was going through, to which I added the disappointment I felt from my teacher at my behaviour. There had been nothing "normal" or standard about it.

Coming back to our days, looking around us or following the fakes transmitted through social media, we encounter a so-called normality. As if anyone can really say what this "normal" means. If so, who set the benchmark? And by what authority? I am not you and you are not me. If you choose to be someone else's "copy" it is only your issue. I just want to be "me", and if you don't accept me it's... your issue, too. "What you think about me is not my problem," says Terry Cole-Whittaker (36).

Doesn't being "normal" mean being the way I am, without trying to be someone else's copy so as not to upset, disturb or disappoint others? If you don't accept me because you don't like me, I can't make you change your attitude and I don't want to, because the expression states "forced love, it's not possible."

I live according to my own beliefs and values because this is the only life I have here and now. So, as long as I'm not causing harm, others shouldn't be concerned about why I think, speak, or act differently. Instead of being disturbed by someone else's choices, it's better to reflect on the reasons for your own discomfort. As the saying goes, "Don't look for the speck of sawdust in your brother's eye when you have a plank in your own."

Hypocrisy

Honestly speaking, dealing with the beam in my eye is easy, especially if you're doing it behind my back. It's also easy to try to manipulate me if you think you need me because hypocrisy is a prevalent issue in our society. Life has allowed me to witness how this weapon is sharpened and grown since the children of small school age, with whom I have worked for over twenty years.

As we well know, a child is like a piece of clay that is shaped by parents, school, and everyone who enters their life. They are like a sponge that absorbs everything they see and hear, in addition to what they inherit and learn from their family.

I particularly remember a little girl who was my student during my last years as a teacher. She was beautiful, talkative like a bird, cheerful, and warm-hearted, and she did everything she could to be surrounded by as many "friends" as possible.

She was beautiful and intelligent, but she was frustrated by the comparison that most people made between her, being "fat," and the other girls. She loved talking to everyone and making jokes with her colleagues. I would see her running from one group to another, carrying stories and telling them to different groups. The message arrived in a different form from one group to another, depending on her "interests" at that age. It was her way of existing and drawing attention to herself in order to be "seen." Unconsciously, she did not see herself as beautiful and valuable, and she sought attention and wanted to be in control, using all the weapons of selfishness at her disposal at that age.

In this way, the false lack of self-worth and the fear of not being seen as the same as or better than others push you to hypocrisy. When I choose to say and do things I don't believe in, just to fit in, I become a hypocrite, and hypocrisy is widespread in our society.

I go back to my memories, and I remember a time from my childhood when, as a 10-year-old girl, I walked home from school alone, as I often did. I was too focused on being fair to everyone, avoiding trouble, and excelling at everything I did. Yet, my peers shunned or laughed at me. I didn't have time for play or laughter. I had to take care of my younger siblings like a "parent," and I spent hours studying because I "must" be very good. I didn't have time for anything else, so books became my best friends.

I walked home from school as I always did, but this time, I tried to avoid the slush formed from the melted snow which filled the alleys between the buildings. Even though I tried to avoid it, I couldn't. The water soaked through my new leather boots, leaving me with frozen feet and tears in my eyes. I cried bitterly, as I had many times before and would many times after. I didn't understand why people lied, why they said one thing and did another without explanation. I couldn't help but wonder, 'Why is the world so bad? What have we done to deserve this? What am I doing wrong because I don't act the way they do?"(46)

It is a way we learn from a young age that the world is hypocritical. Unhappy with ourselves and our lives, we find fault with everything we or others do. We look for ways to draw attention to ourselves because that's how worthless we are. On the other hand, if you are honest or try to be honest, you will realize that in this society, where, as Okakura Kakuzo says, "good and truth" are bartered (29), you are seen as a "fool" or a victim. In order not to feel like that, you also adopt the "norms" of society, trying to respect its patterns. However, you hide how you feel by resorting to insincerity or false sincerity.

This hypocrisy is present everywhere, but it reaches its highest levels in politics and religion. I refer to them again because they are the institutions that most strongly instil fear and manipulate people.

Those who commit the worst crimes that you may never have thought of are defenders of justice. The biggest liars hide behind titles and honours. Those who destroy the environment become advocates for ecology. The biggest criminals are hidden under the brand of "blue blood" and rights as sovereigns. Among the wealthiest individuals on the planet are often the biggest hypocrites who claim to "save" people from poverty and disease. In their concern for the benefits they bring to humanity, they get rich from the poison that is an ingredient in food, an element of water purification, from medicines and products of questionable quality, in "2+1 free" offers.

Hypocrisy is at home when we talk about religions and the church. Religions preach love between people, but their adherents curse you, shun you, or ask you to be put aside if you don't believe what they believe or do what, when, and how they do. Religion? Fanaticism and cruelty, Oliver Sacks calls it, when after admitting his sexual orientation, his mother, a religious woman, told him to his face that she wished she had never given birth to him.

Many who attend churches are saints at the mercy of icons and "devils" when someone does not act according to the patterns in which they live.

I remember a scene that happened many years ago, inside a church when he was waiting in line for anafura.

A pale, pregnant woman, who caught my eye when I saw her enter the church, poorly dressed, is stopped by a "lady" who begins to question her vehemently, who, when, and how and also gives her a hard time (there in the church) because she was a great sinner by being pregnant without being married. (Hi, Hi!) My conclusion was that they knew each other. The pale woman answered all lady's required answers while trying to move forward a little because she really wanted to talk to the priest. That lady, well-dressed, and elegant, prostrates herself in front of the priest, starting to praise his priestly skills in the service. The pregnant woman had tried several times to get the priest's attention once she got near him, but he was too absorbed in the lady's praise. Even if she waited, you could feel her fear of not losing the priest because she "desperately" wanted to talk to him.

After the eulogies are over, the "man of God" turns to the pale woman and screams, "WHAT DO YOU WANT?" in the "house of God".

Isn't a priest who preaches about loving one's neighbour but doesn't embrace poverty and humility a hypocrite? Does a priest who holds grudges against his mother for worldly reasons and doesn't seek her until her death truly love his neighbour? Isn't it hypocritical for him and those with him to take money from those who see them as a conduit to heaven? How can they sell health, eternal life, and happiness for money when they preach love and the fear of money as the "eye of the devil," yet eagerly collect as much as possible and share with those who help them collect it or as a "bonus" for the "highest" ones rank than them? Do they need opulent clothes and ornaments to preach? Do you really need to stand out with such things, if your heart is pure, and as a plus, you are a "man of God"? Doesn't the saying "do what the pope says, not what he does" stem from such behaviour?

Aren't the increasingly lavish churches and ornate decorations built with the "devil's eye" in mind? If one wishes to worship, you can do it in your house, in the mud or a field, in grass and amongst flowers. You don't need pompous, gilded, ornate buildings when that money or fenced land could be used to help those who have no shelter, food, or clothing."

Is he, not a hypocrite because he preaches the love of his neighbour but looks down on the one who does not have or does not want to put money in the "plate" that accompanies him? He is also a hypocrite because he arrogates to himself the right to punish people with "psalms" and such prayers that they pay for by buying them from churches. Even the candles must be made of "the wax from the church they serve" because the others are not "sanctified". Sanctified with hypocrisy or does the candle burn only from the exact address? Are sins counted according to the wax of the candle? The church?! A temple of hypocrisy.

A hypocrite is every person who gossips about another by exploring their "sins". Hypocrisy is at home in our society. We are hypocrites because we do not want to take responsibility for what is happening around us. We are waiting for "someone else" to do it. You throw the paper on the road, but let the cleaner pick it up. You throw garbage into the water, but let those who take care of it collect it.

Hypocritical is every existing law in the states because they are made to chain the one who crushes himself by working, to favour the one who sits in an office and "cuts leaves to the dogs" while counting the money taken from the many. A hypocrite is every man who knows what he knows and prefers to remain silent. He waits for another to do something for him and the rest, although each of us is an "other" for the rest...

Wherever you turn your eyes, you will see hypocrisy. It is present in the family, between parents and children, where the parent says one thing and does another. It is present between siblings, where there is a fierce struggle for inheritance. Whenever you look, it is everywhere and alive, and its greatest power is supported by money and the false power of selfishness.

False Assumption

Hypocrisy immediately leads to false assumptions. We tend to assume what might benefit us personally, disregarding the assumption that can also lead to suffering. Selfishness avoids acknowledging this suffering and prefers to stay locked up tight because suffering means pain.

The assumption is false because we do not "take heart in our teeth" for our actions and their consequences. Instead, we easily assume everything that is not ours, that does not belong to us and that we did not get through our work. From simple drawings, and images posted on the Internet that we use as if they are our own and do not give credit to the creator, we continue with literary creations which do not belong to us and end up with houses, smaller or larger plots of land, forests and businesses, the life work of some, or valuables belonging to other nations, to the grabbing of other nations' territories. The one that swallows everything that can be of external value, everything that can be converted into money, is the greatest enemy of this society. It is the "demon" in everyone and it is called EGOISM.

When you fail to take responsibility for your own thoughts, words, deeds, or appropriate that is not the fruit of your creation and labour, you are indulging in selfish behaviour and making false assumptions. Claiming that you have not been or are not selfish is a lie that you give to yourself and others, only that this society is made of all of us and at the same time, we are each a part of the puzzle of this world. Each of us is responsible for our "piece" of humanity's consciousness.

If my words upset you, that's your issue to address. Take a deep look within yourself and understand the source of your anger.

Disappointment

Out of hypocrisy or not, we often develop expectations that can easily lead us to disappointment. In fact, our expectations are essentially our thoughts linked to certain emotions. If it happens as we want, it is natural that we will be happy, but if it does not happen, we will become disappointed, we will feel struck by fate, or punished by a god. If we take into consideration the advice from C. S. Lewis's book (7), when experiences make us feel happy, what is material is true, and in the case of experiences that bring us disappointments, we look for the spiritual side...

In reality, by constantly expecting certain outcomes, we inadvertently create a conditioned way of life for ourselves. Yet, disappointment also stems from our past, and can manifest as anger, sadness, crying or aggression. We create expectations for both ourselves and others.

Expecting responses to your words or actions from those with whom you are trying to communicate, you may easily be disappointed when they do not respond. Even though they likely have their own reasons for not replying, we take their lack of communication directly and personally as a personal affront. At the same time, the reason for not responding, beyond forgetfulness, goes back to the inherent selfishness in humanity. It is its hunger to demonstrate its power and false worth that it does not find otherwise.

A response can be a refusal if that's what you want to do. The decision change can be as simple as saying "I changed my decision" or "I don't want it anymore". But like everything else, the choice of how to proceed is up to each individual. Everyone offers what they have.

You can also feel disappointed when someone rejects your advice or guidance, but that person will do what they know, what they want, and what they can. There is no need to be disappointed because we live in a society where most people have advice for everyone in every field, we know everything for everyone, yet we often don't know much about ourselves. We don't really know ourselves, but we think we know others very well.

When it comes to love in a relationship, you might be disappointed because your partner is not giving you love in the way you imagine they should. He doesn't meet your expectations. However, have you ever wondered if you really know your partner and yourself well enough? We say we know our partners, but if I am disappointed with myself in many situations in life, how can I not be disappointed with my partner or others around me? Those around us are like our mirrors. Not knowing these things, you might conclude that your partner does not love you as much as you do, in other words, you love selfishly.

Love knows no evaluation, has no terms of comparison, it just exists. In true love, we appreciate every moment spent with the other person without having any expectations. True love is like offering a flower because you genuinely feel that way, not because your mind dictated "it should", "this is how it is done", "this is good and beautiful", "it is X day". The more you seek to prove to someone the love you have for them, the greater it can stem out the fear that directs you. The less trust you have in the love you have for that person, and the less trust you have in the love your partner has for you. Without trust, love is fake on one side or the other...or both.

Giving something to the person you say you love just to prove it to them, out of fear of being rejected, of being alone, of being abandoned, of losing a love that you think it's yours for life, you do it out of fear. Expectations of any kind can stem from selfishness, from the fear of not being good enough, valuable, and it is natural that you will experience disappointments.

Parents whose children do not live up to the standards they set are also disappointed. They don't even think how selfish they (we) are when we condition our children, when we ask them to do what we want. Under the slogan "I am your parent and I know what is best for you", we force our children to live the dreams that we had and did not find the courage to fulfil. We force our children to attend the schools we choose under the same slogan without knowing or even having the idea that the children's wishes need our respect. Sometimes, even if we know them, we don't appreciate them, we consider them insignificant because they have no value in a society full of "values". We cannot accept that our child will not become "someone" if we did not do it or failed. We believe that pointing them in a certain direction, they will be happier, without considering that our parents did the same with us, and many of us are still living unhappy lives. We do not take into account that for any being, even if it is our child, to decide what he wants to do with his life is his prerogative and not the parents' prerogative to impose by force, as Richard Dawkins says (35).

Returning to the quiver of memories, I remember a story from one of my jobs in London. A young colleague told me that his parents had forced him to attend a certain college, even though he didn't want to. He graduated but refused to work in that field because he didn't enjoy it. He felt that the years spent in college were a waste of his life, but he didn't want to disappoint his parents. (46)

Everything we do to meet others' expectations can lead to disappointment and a life that doesn't align with our true desires, causing and deepening our inner pain.

These disappointments, born like many other "weapons" from fears; fears of worthlessness, weakness, lack of direction, judgment, ridicule or disappointments, teach us valuable lessons to overcome obstacles and change the direction of our lives.

Mockery

Using the "weapons" of fear leads to increased selfishness, and in order to reinforce the belief that it is strong and maintains its power, it will employ all possible means provided by the mind.

Ridicule, subtle mockery or scorn, which does not mean joy, but is the opposite of it, is also part of the "weapons of fear". It does not sharpen the mind nor support the affection of those involved. It is a weapon that we use against others, to release our accumulated frustrations because we feel cornered by our lack of worth, we feel insignificant or weak. By using ridicule, individuals seek to regain a sense of control in the face of perceived loss caused by selfishness, as it creates the illusion of dominating others. However, this behaviour essentially stems from selfishness, as it feeds on the emotional "destruction" of the perceived weaknesses in others, without realising that it only serves to mock one's own lack of understanding and inner pain, and spread negativity into the world.

It's important not to mistake ridicule for gentle irony or good-natured teasing, including when directed at oneself, which we choose to do it for genuine fun.

Love does not resort to ridicule. It acknowledges that each person is unique and has the right to make their own choices. Every choice carries consequences, and making choices also involves accepting their outcomes.

Cowardice

Driven by the fear of being wrong, or ridiculed, our egoism resorts to whatever tricks it can find to achieve its goals. If by false procrastination we seek false pleasure in something else than what we have begun or wish to begin, by cowardice we seek to attain our ends. Thus, we also trample on the dust of confidence that we still have in us. We often believe that the confidence we seek from others will help us gain self-confidence, but it is just another facet of lying, a lie, as is everything born of selfishness. Falsity.

Cowardice can be viewed as a form of indirect self-hatred. The more cowardice we exhibit, the more we end up hating ourselves and others leading to increased inner suffering, says C. S. Lewis (7), and through that, it tries to compensate for the miseries of fears.

Due to our unconscious belief in our worthlessness, our minds consider it a weakness and we cling to cowardice to "lie" to ourselves that we are worthy. By displaying cowardice, we may see ourselves as strong when around those we admire or follow, believing that we benefit. Still resorting to this cowardice, we consider ourselves safe from danger. This can lead us to refrain from expressing our opinions or providing subtle messages to make those "important" understand that we show them the respect we think they deserve. Out of fear, we are the ones who don't respect ourselves. We may even try to support what we perceive as valuable in others to feel valuable ourselves, along with them.

Out of cowardice, we may fail to demand the rights that we are entitled to as humans and choose to live in a state of comfort that we desire to change, yet hope others will do it for us.

Indifference

Sitting in our comfort zone, we often ignore our desires and let them fade away like a flower, choosing to do anything else that doesn't require us to leave that comfort. By not listening to our intuition, we allow our fears to control us and weigh more heavily on us than our desires. We silence our intuition and push away its whispers, burying them in a corner of our soul with the intention of forgetting them, only to feel regret later. As Okakura Kakuzo says, "Nothing is sadder than to see a withered flower mercilessly thrown on a rubbish heap" (29).

We give up on our desires easily because we give up a little bit of ourselves every day, and we come up with all kinds of reasons to justify it, because unconsciously, our value is too little or non-existent. Our minds will split the thread into many other threads to fabricate reasons to make us believe that we are indifferent to anything that could cause us suffering. In reality, we don't believe in our desires because we don't believe in ourselves and our worth. Each time we do this, we add more weight to our emotional baggage, suffocating our souls. Expressions like "my soul is breaking" or "my soul is heavy" might resonate with you. These phrases capture what we experience, yet we often overlook our own well-being and let our souls wither like a flower under the weight of the "garbage" of our selfishness.

In this way, the concept of indifference is often used as a shield to protect ourselves from emotional pain. We may try to convince ourselves and others that we are not affected by their words or actions, but deep down, suffering is a natural part of human experience. We cannot simply ignore or suppress our emotions, as they will resurface eventually, often in unexpected ways because without pain, without suffering, no wound knows healing.

I was told many times "be more indifferent", "learn not to hurt yourself". As if you can dictate to your lower self how to behave or your soul not to love. You do what you feel, you do what you think, what you know, you can and want. And yet how far can you go with false indifference? Until you reach depression, you drown yourself in drugs or alcohol because you "want to forget". "don't you want to know", "don't you want to feel"? And yet you feel, because we are not born to be "with lack of feelings". We are born to feel and allow ourselves to experience our emotions. By suppressing them, you are not becoming indifferent, you are lying to yourself and you will experience the repercussions anyway, sooner or later. The mask you will display, the indifference, will only remain false. In another place, towards other people you will discharge the anger inside you because you did not take a stand at a certain moment, because you suppressed your emotions too much to pretend indifference. Emotions need to be released, it's not for nothing that we say "I feel like I'm exploding, if not..."

By using indifference to demonstrate the lack of pain we think we will make others feel pain with this indifference. It's just that "home calculation doesn't match the one at the market". It is possible that the person to whom you want to prove that they did not affect you by their words or actions, is not bothered by your attitude at all. But the one who will be on the same vibration as your condition will react or suffer in turn.

In addition to the type of false indifference mentioned earlier, some display indifference caused by ignorance. One of the most dramatic aspects of the human condition is the connection between ignorance and pride, expressed so well by the Romanian saying "The stupid is not stupid enough, if it's not also proud."

Looking for the definition of ignorance, we find it as "lack of knowledge, lack of teaching." Carlos Castaneda (6) says that it is ignorance that compels us to abandon everything that does not align with the expectations of our self-image. I won't delve into the debate about the meaning of ignorance, but we can think of those who, as I mentioned earlier, have limited formal education yet manage life's problems much better than others with more schooling. Learning "per se" arises from the curiosity to know, to learn, and you do it because it interests you and helps you achieve a goal related to what you enjoy, not because someone else asks or forces you to do it. Moreover, if you wish, you can learn from others, from animals, nature, and anywhere. When you don't want to, you pretend not to see; when you're afraid, you bury yourself in ignorance, as Patricia Cori says.

Born and bred of fear, it became the reason humanity was kept so long in darkness, for ignorance is the darkness in which we stand chained by fear, or as the Emerald Tablets of Thoth the Atlantean say, "Learning is considered ignorance by foolish people, and profitable things are harmful to them. They live in death, and this is their food." (40)

We often ignore the well-being of people, trees, and animals out of fear of getting hurt or because, unconsciously, we feel too small, and insignificant to make a difference. It is easier to cling to the familiar darkness and yearn for the light than to actively pursue knowledge and enlightenment.

How much truth is there in the words "he's stupid, but he's happy"? Ignorance is not bliss. The choice of the few to keep many in ignorance, to keep their faces out, because of the effects of knowledge, is compared by W.W. Atkinson (38) to giving a man permission to smoke, when he sits on a powder keg, instead of explaining to him about the explosive or, advising him to bury his head in the sand like an ostrich, than to know and watch the approach of danger.

Ignorance prevails whenever we lack self-awareness or fail to stand up for our "so-called rights". Ignorance is "at home" where women and children are treated as "property", where our actions pollute waters, and where forests vanish. Asking "What to do?", do you answer "I'm small and powerless"? Your answer exposes your lack of self-confidence or self-awareness. Your words really prove how small you see yourself on the inside, how lacking in self-confidence you are, how weak you see yourself in front of others, or how ignorant you are. We all have power; it's up to us to either give it away through our beliefs or use it ourselves.

Ignorance is not a safety net against anything. It strips us of any connection with our own being and our own life so that we can live as we wish. It is not for nothing that the symbol of human ignorance is a demon, on which the god Shiva is depicted dancing, and liberation comes when that demon is removed.

Living with the family of selfishness that comes with the courage we condition and the desire not to suffer, indifference rears its head as an emotional supplement. However, we are not indifferent. The soul is not indifferent. Everything that provokes emotions in us either moves our energy in a beneficial direction or not. We change our vibration and at the same time leave our energetic imprint on others.

Thus, just as a stone thrown into water propagates waves, so the waves of our vibrations change the face of the world.

I recall a beautiful autumn day when I walked to the shopping centre in the city. A woman, seemingly my age, threw her food wrapper on the cobblestones, even though a trash can was nearby. She had passed the trash can by a few meters, and the next one was several tens of meters away. I asked her if she thought it would be better to throw the packaging in the bin and showed her where the nearest one was. She looked at me dumbfounded and slowly, she bent down, picked up the package and threw it in the bin. So, we can take a stand if we care about what's happening and want to make a difference. Of course, not every situation works out smoothly. I have been verbally abused before for speaking up. But in other cases, when I couldn't confront the person, I picked up the trash and disposed of it. I didn't feel like garbage worker or worthless. I was glad I did something good for the planet. (46)

With every attitude, the wave that goes out into the universe changes something. Every thought and every deed changes the vibrational frequency around us. Then should I remain indifferent or do something good?

If you are indifferent to the one who throws papers and plastic bottles on the road, on the beach, or in the waters, it is not false indifference. It is ignorance. The expression "let someone else collect it" because they are paid to do it, belongs to selfishness. No one owes you to pick up your trash. Just as you (I suppose) clean your kitchen table after you have prepared food or after eating, so it is necessary to clean the place in nature where you pass. You drink water from the waters where you throw your filth. From the ground where you throw your garbage, fruits, vegetables, and animals grow that end up on your table. You don't know or... you don't want to know?

Deliberate indifference or not, it is disrespect for your being and the rest of the world. Do we want the world to look different? Then we are not and cannot be indifferent to what is happening around us, with our peers or with nature.

Both the wise and the ignorant are subject to the same laws that govern the Universe, says the Kybalion (39). The difference is that the wise is a skilful swimmer who goes and comes in all directions, while the ignorant is but a log carried by the current of water in all directions. Similarly, Lao Tze says that ignorant people fear that they are insignificant, but "Superior people, when they hear about the Tao, put it into practice"; the people at the bottom sometimes follow, sometimes they ignore; the inferior and stupid, however, they laugh." (18)

False Security

Many times, we use false indifference not out of genuine concern for others, but we care about the "neighbour's goat" because we don't know what to do with our time and life, or we consider that we are doing someone a favour for their safety, although we do not know what good he wants.

I told in the previous book about my return to the native country after working abroad for many years (45). Since returning, it has happened to me many times, that different people who know me, give me advice to return to education. I understand that their advice comes from their desire to do me a favour and it sounds something like this: "Go back to education, because you have a job and a secure income".

Is it really so? Can anyone say what is certain in this world? Can anyone guarantee that they will live to see tomorrow, keep their job until retirement, or stay in the same relationship for life?

What defines security? Who bestows it upon us? Some argue that true security comes from money, but does it really? "If you have money" you are sure because you have something to put your hands on. True, you have something to comfort. Its primary role is to facilitate transactions, not serve as a false conversion for human worth. The size of one's bank account, the grandeur of their home, or the make of their car may command respect in a selfish society, but money itself holds no intrinsic value. We have not yet discovered any seed from which money trees will grow with coins and paper currency instead of leaves and fruits, but our selfishness shows how much respect we have for those papers/metal to the detriment of man and nature.

False security, which is actually insecurity, leads us to seek anchors such as finding a well-paying job or a partner with a good appearance or a good financial situation. Even if they don't meet these standards, at least we have someone by our side so that we don't feel "alone".

Living with a false sense of security is because we lack visible evidence of true security. Did you know that prolonged insecurity can result in physical conditions in the stomach area and the lumbosacral spine? People who have had or now have sciatic nerve problems are often the most worried about financial insecurity in their lives. The fear of insecurity in the future leads to disappointment and anxiety, affecting everything related to movement, the nervous system, as well as the arms and legs.

Insecurity causes you to constantly seek confirmation in everything you do to boost your self-worth. It also leads you to look for faults in others or blame yourself for failures. As a result, you may be inclined to sacrifice self-respect and embrace servitude. Additionally, you may find yourself apologising for mistakes that aren't necessarily yours. Insecurity makes you view weakness as a fundamental error.

Insecurity, or false security, has been present throughout human history, stemming from the false sense of value associated with money. The only true security lies within us, within our souls. All you need to do is believe in yourself and follow your intuition. It's from this place of inner security that you'll find solutions to any challenges life presents, and you'll come to accept that every experience you encounter is ultimately for your own benefit. When others offer advice or guidance, it's important to remember that their perspective and experiences shape their understanding of what's best for you. While their intentions are good, they do not truly understand what "your good" entails.

Take what resonates with you from their advice, but ultimately, you are the one responsible for defining what is "best for you".

Resignation

Seeking false security that you delude yourself to find, even though it is only temporary, in external things or the people around you, you will experience disappointment taken to two extremes. One is resignation, and the other is depression with all that can follow from it. Both are easy to reach when we let fear direct our suffering because, in the worries of everyday life, we find what C. S. Lewis calls "direct assistance" (7).

We call for resignation when we feel dominated by others and try to follow the "normalization" of society. By resigning, we give up on expressing our thoughts and actions. We don't want to show that our opinions are completely different, so as not to "upset" or disturb. We may hesitate due to insecurity, but once we decide to quit, it becomes resignation. We do this to avoid upsetting or making another person "feel bad". We prefer to make ourselves feel bad for not speaking up or taking the desired action. It's as if we accept that giving up on ourselves is very normal because we live like we are not worthy. We hesitate to express our knowledge and feelings to avoid deviating from societal "standards", leading to resignation for shorter or longer periods, or even for life.

We often struggle to come to terms with the inevitability of death, whether it's the passing of someone we've known for a short or long time. We understand that life leads to death. Is it resignation or a lack of understanding about death? Do we fail to honestly accept that we are only passing through this life, entering it only to eventually leave? Life, in essence, can be likened to a room with two entrances, as described by Carlos Castaneda (6). We enter through one entrance and depart through the other. Should we resign ourselves to this fact or strive to understand and genuinely accept it?

Resignation involves falsely accepting that we cannot have the things we desire or believe we don't deserve them. Our selfish pursuit of these things stems from a desire to appear superior to others. Pursuing something because it satisfies our desires coming from the heart does not aim to display a non-existent value, but allows us to express our individuality, uniqueness, and authenticity. It is what each of us has.

Sincere acceptance of whatever life gives us arises from gentleness and humility and should not be confused with resignation. Surrendering without understanding what we have buried inside us only adds to the inner emotional baggage, which can become a lid over an active volcano. This unresolved turmoil can erupt unexpectedly, causing those around us to become the victims of unexpressed and unaddressed anger.

Fake responsibility

Accustomed to resign ourselves, we give up on ourselves, on our intuition, for what is "normal" in society and thus we end up assuming false responsibility.

The best example that makes its way among the memories are the petitions that I sent years ago to different ministries and only one of them responded each time. Where is the responsibility of those elected to lead a nation, people, responsibility that is part of their job? Do they prioritize their own interests over their duty to the public? It is propagated the idea that there is no economic growth, that there is no money in the budget for schools and hospitals, for roads. Yet, there always seems to be money available for their own interests because they take false responsibility. With all the leaflets and election campaigns, conferences and congresses, they "change their hair, but their temper, no". I honestly feel very sorry for them. For all their wealth, their actions, the playing of people who care about the community, they prove one thing: they are completely irresponsible because they were and are unloving beings.

Our thoughts, emotions, and actions belong to us, and true responsibility lies in owning them, along with the consequences they bring. Responsibility is not only individual but collective, as each person is part of the world and influences it with their choices. There is no responsibility of mine only for "me", and of others for "the rest of the world", because each of the "rest of the world" is an "I" that is part of the "rest of the world" for another "I". Everyone's thoughts and emotions are reflected in our actions and change the world for worse or better, and the decision to be responsible or not belongs to each of us.

As always, we can take lessons from nature. The sun does not make exceptions in lighting the planet, and the earth does not divide us to give us shelter for our existence.

Despair

Even though we don't truly own anything in this world, our education and experiences often lead us to believe that we are owners of houses, land, and wealth, as well as power over the lives of others. This false sense of dominion exists because of selfishness.

We are taught to attach ourselves to material things in pursuit of illusory happiness. As a result, we become desperate when we can't acquire that certain "something" we believe will make us happy. What's more, we are misled into thinking that we can "possess" other people and that their lives should conform to our desires. This false attachment leads us to despair, a state that, as C.S. Lewis suggests, leads to a squeezed and drained soul (7).

Strong emotional bonds are known to be a basic component of human nature, and attachment is an enduring psychological connection between human beings that refers to intimate and emotional bonds we form with others.

Aside from human attachment, we have also mistakenly attached ourselves to material possessions such as money, houses, and cars. This leads to despair when we fail to achieve our goals and attempt to enforce our desires. The negativity that feeds this fear, as Doreen Virtue mentions (11), can nullify hours of positive affirmations, and our fear can manifest as a negative prayer that attracts the fulfilment of our "prophecies."

The concept of false attachment is rooted in our childhood experiences. Those who have experienced lack tend to become attached to many objects. This attachment is driven by the fear of scarcity. For example, when we make or buy more food than we can eat, it stems from a fear of hunger and poverty that we may not even be aware of. This false attachment style dictates our perception of "happiness".

In my book "Recipe for Happiness," I confess that for a long time I was fixated on "academic diplomas" (45). I lived by the "if, then I will get..." This expression"if... then..." was part of me because I knew how to live by conditioning myself. Each thing obtained created for me the illusory state of temporary happiness, which then disappeared, leaving room for another game to bring me the much-desired happiness. This is because the ego is not satisfied, but continually hungry and dissatisfied. Being insatiable, it is always seeking more. Being false it is chasing after a false happiness.

We find ourselves in a constant rush to acquire things that we believe will make us happy. As a result, we end up with a house full of objects that we don't have space for and clothes that we hardly ever wear. Therefore, closets are full of clothes, although many are forgotten for a long time. We also seek validation and acquire "friends" on social networks in an attempt to find meaning and value because the idea of much, means value. We run and develop obsessions for a false value.

In everything we collect, be it clothes, objects or "false friends", we are desperately searching for value. A value that we no longer know where to look for. However, it is "just a click" away from our being. It's where we weren't taught to look. It is in us, in our souls, where the real light is. Looking in the outer world, says Thoth the Atlantean, "man only lives in darkness, the light of the great fire being hidden within himself". (40)

Understanding that this false attachment stems from our childhood traumas and memories, enables us to identify, comprehend, and acknowledge its existence within us. However, we do not need to hold onto it any longer, as it impedes us from living life authentically. We must acknowledge that we are deceiving ourselves, and instead strive to live a simple, beautiful, and happy life. The external desires that stem from this false attachment only create an illusion of happiness, while fostering selfishness.

The initial attachment to loved ones, became possessive of objects and persons and fuelled by selfishness, led us to despair of obtaining them. Today, despair is also present in relationships with loved ones because whatever we do, we don't end up receiving a true "moment of love" from them. Too caught up in the material world, by the pains we live in, in the world we create based on the negative thoughts fed by the media, we don't make time for ourselves. Consequently, we search for affection outside ourselves, we have "time" for others. This desperation for affection has become the cancer of our society, where many find solace in drink, sex, drugs, violence. We are looking for "a moment of love" and we have no idea that it is always inside us, not outside.

Our fixation on rationality has led us to neglect our inner world, and we have made it seem more and more ephemeral, because as humans we have given up knowing without words as Carlos Castaneda says (6), when in fact the soul does not need anything from the outside, because it has everything we need to be happy.

Victimization

It's important to understand that by recognizing and addressing our traumas, we can gain insight into our lived experiences and why we may have fallen into a pattern of victimhood. Reflecting on our past can help us understand the reasons behind our behaviours and feelings of guilt or the tendency to look for a culprit outside and blame others. However, holding onto these feelings does not help us free from our past and move forward.

Living as a victim most of our lives is normal these days because we don't dare to stand like a tree in the storm for our opinions and rights. We appeal to our false defence which is victimization, becoming a "victim of society", although society is also us. We are the victims of our partners, although we chose them. We are victims of our children, even though we boast that we conceived and raised them. To feel the victims of someone else is like feeling the victims of pears falling from the tree on our head, when in fact, as Arthur Schopenhauer says (5) "Everyone on earth carries the punishment of his existence, as a result of his way of being." We are ultimately victims of our own mindset, and it's within our power to change our thoughts.

While writing this, I'm reminded of a magazine from my elementary school days that I really enjoyed. It was simple and beautifully illustrated, featuring educational stories with characters like Donald Duck and Mickey Mouse. In one story, one of them couldn't learn anything at school, and the other found the ideal solution for him. To get the knowledge into his mind, he put a funnel to his ear and began to pour the contents of the pages into his head.

Similarly, we allow others to feed our minds and our fears with what we accept as good from what "pops into our heads". However, as humans, we have the alternative to filter the information and seek other sources. It is said that certain information does not reach us for nothing. The universe sends us what we need; it's just that we decide whether we want to use it or not. We alone decide whether we want to change our way of thinking or not.

When you feel like a victim, you really are a victim, only of your thoughts based on the fears you have. Victimization is just another weapon your mind uses to respond to the fear of not being good enough or not being worthy. Moreover, when we keep complaining from a victim position, we only recreate the aspects we complain about. By not taking action to change something, it means that we are feeding them to come back because we don't have enough of them and how long we have lived them. Victimization or self-pity is your enemy that gives you false worth to maintain your self-importance. But in the fight against selfishness, self-importance needs to be dethroned, as Carlos Castaneda (6) says. We do it when we look for its origins and learn that we can choose between remaining hapless victims or becoming powerful beings.

Everyone has their own fears and traumas. These experiences shape our beliefs and behaviours, and often stem from our childhood. Each person's unique life experiences have led them to where they are today. No one can do exactly what you do in the same way because we all have our own individual skills. No one is better or worse, we are just different.

Whenever you fail to meet your expectations or reach the point where you resort to false assumption, needing confirmation, you do it again out of fear of not being good enough. We are the ones who need to truly understand that the real change of all of us begins from within each of us.

From the subconscious where you have stored traumas, no matter how much you want to live another life, you will not succeed to truly move forward until you confront and release them. Until we understand, accept, and forgive the related experiences, it's difficult to create a different reality.

You may think that if you just put in more effort or approached things differently, you could achieve your goals. However, the universe doesn't operate on our timeline; it acts when the time is right for us. It is not selfish. It abundantly provides cosmic energy, and the only thing that holds us back is our own thoughts and emotions. Moreover, the more you feel sorry for something, the deeper you sink into looking for solutions, looking for blame, victimizing yourself, but regrets will not alter the situation you are in, they will not change you and they won't change your past.

The soul knows no regrets, recognizing that challenges are part of life's process and lead us towards spiritual growth. It understands that every experience contributes to finding balance and harmony. To achieve this, we need to weigh the knowledge received through the information that reaches us, and on the other side the action we can take to use the knowledge gained. Ultimately, the choices we make belong to us.

4. Thoughts, Words and Deeds

Just as lightning brings forth light, and from light comes thunder and pouring fire, so does man's thought pass into his speech and then into his actions. So remember this: there must be light and thunder before the burning fire. The light of man is his thought, and this is his most precious possession. The light gains strength through words, and the will of man ignites the fire through which everything around him is made.

The Laws of Zamolxis (41)

People think, talk, and act. Oftentimes, our words and actions can differ from our thoughts. We may say or do something that doesn't align with what we truly think or do. However, it feels good when our thoughts are reflected in our words and actions, as it means we are following our inner light.

Although the subconscious and the conscious are one, meaning our mind, it is our subconscious that defines us. Most mental activities are performed unconsciously because some cannot be consciously controlled, while others become automatic and exist in both conscious and unconscious realms, according to Dan Farcaş (8). This explains why most of our actions are automatic. We don't make them consciously, and I also consciously have them stored in my mind. We don't even know what we have stored in our subconscious until we "dig" in, and from my own experience I say that you can be amazed by what you will bring to the surface. You will be amazed at the traumas, the memories, the pains you have accumulated, the length and depth of their existence.

From the emotional confessions of the individuals I've worked with, many have expressed surprise at the things they uncover, saying, "I didn't know that I still had something like that in my mind, it's been so long." It may seem curious and yet it is true. Each of us is actually the sum of beliefs formed on what we have stored in our subconscious. There are no other influences in our world than those we create with our minds because we believe in them, and it is belief that directs the flow of our creation, or as Neville Goddard says, "The subconscious mind is the universal conductor that the operator modifies with his thoughts and feelings"(27). We are what we believe.

In order to change the world, we must first change ourselves. We have been living for too long consumed by feelings of worthlessness, fear, and darkness. We need to change our way of thinking to bring change in the world. Our thoughts reflect our care for everyone and everything around us, including the earth that gives us everything we need to live our lives on this visit to the planet.

If we are not true to our commitments, we cannot expect others to be responsible for their words and actions towards us. We should not demand from others what we are unwilling to give. Failing to keep promises will ultimately hurt us the most, as we receive what we give. When we neglect our own commitments, we also fail to respect others. Just as you don't keep your word to yourself when you decide to change something in your life and procrastinate, you do the same to others, because when you don't respect yourself, you don't respect others either. When we make excuses for our actions, we are not being honest with ourselves. Consequently, can we be honest with others? Moreover, you'll only end up feeling guilty about yourself. You will find fault with yourself or others by resorting to blame, you will seek false forgiveness, or you will give up on forgiveness as well. By using fake forgiveness, you revert to irresponsibility. By consciously reneging on commitments, the guilt is removed, but by making it a habit to quit, you'll be the first to pay the price. We only reap what we sow...

When we fight each other, we are essentially fighting ourselves because we are all interconnected energy. The ego often leads us to believe that we have power over others, judging what is good and bad. However, these qualities exist within each of us to varying degrees. Although, we often think that what we do for others is for their own good, where is the love? How do we know that the good we see will bring good to another? Do we truly understand what is best for them? Have we considered that they may not want or need what we are offering, or perhaps they are not ready to receive it? It is often driven by selfishness that we expect others to think, feel, or act as we do.

Acting out of genuine love means respecting others' personal boundaries and choices. We respect them because we respect each other. No one has the right to manipulate us just for the sake of his truth. No one has the right to judge us, criticize us or control our lives. We each have the right to decide our own actions, because everyone has the right to live their lives as they want, as they can, as they know best for them. Furthermore, we often comply with others' requests out of fear and lack of self-belief, reluctant to refuse out of fear of the consequences. We need to see that we have the option to tell "no" and making any decision comes with taking responsibility for it, along with the consequences that follow from it.

Most of the time we do what is asked of us because we don't have the drive to do otherwise. We are afraid to tell "no" to parents, teachers, managers because we are afraid to assume the consequences of a refusal. We don't believe in this option, because we don't believe in ourselves or we don't know we have this alternative of refusal.

Cleaning up my emotions has been a tough journey. One of the most challenging things I've learned is to start saying "no" to others. Yet, following our soul's voice often begins with learning to tell the word to those around us. It's a way of setting our own boundaries and respecting our personal space and freedom.

Sometimes we're inclined to do forbidden things. For instance, a child may jump into the pool even though they were told not to, or someone may seek drugs despite being warned against it. It begs the question: do we want to challenge the authority of those trying to control our lives? Do we seek revenge? Or do we desire the freedom to take charge of our lives? Understanding that we have the freedom to choose our actions and take responsibility for the consequences allows us to experience a sense of "freedom," as we liberate ourselves from the chains of fear.

Acting with the expectation of a reward is insincere. It's a selfish act driven by self-interest because you do it for benefit. Actions that are not rooted in genuine goodwill often lead to disappointment and frustration, as these are also consequences of our actions from which you reap what you sow. By sowing hatred, discord and malice, you will not reap love, because by sowing selfishness, you will reap its fruits. You will receive love when you sow it, but its seeds, even if they want to, will not be able to bear fruit if you have chosen to sweep the traumas like garbage under the rug. Love can only be cultivated when we actively sow it. They will bear fruit on a land from which you have cleared through acceptance and healing, the traumas. As we change, we'll experience the effect of our actions in a different changing world because we are the ones changing.

With and without mask

The impact of our actions is evident in everyday life, which can be likened to a masquerade ball, with everyone wearing one or even multiple masks. Schopenhauer (5) compares the world to a bog, observing that those who reach old age have witnessed the same show multiple times and are no longer surprised by life's offerings. He says that in the first forty years, we write texts, then spend the next thirty years seeking the moral of life, and finally, as the end approaches, all masks fall. It is only then that we see we have nothing and no one to hide from and how falsely we have lived.

We wear masks to portray a false image that conforms to societal norms, and for hiding our true feelings of anger, ignorance, fear, and greed, or even allowing them to surface. As Schopenhauer states, "Men are like the moon and the hunchbacks: they show but one face; they have the innate gift of using their physiognomy as a mask, expressing what is useful to them at the time."(5)

Some masks are perceived as more "beautiful" or important than others, and we tend to favour those instead the beings who try not to wear them and be themselves. Do we really not believe that there is still goodness, sincerity and truth in ourselves and in others?

A closer look reveals the prevalence of falsehood around us. From the artificial things we accumulate over years to the false sense of worth that stems from external alterations to our bodies, injected or encrusted. Yet, if we stand crooked and look straight into our soul, we may understand that our pursuit of external adjustments is driven by a lack of self-worth as humans. So, if you do not have the belief that you are worthy, do you think you will have it by adding something else brought from the outside into you or on you?

We often use the term "common man" to refer to some of our peers, based on societal norms. The interpretation of this term varies depending on who is using it and how. Those who consider themselves of higher social status or "blue blood" often use the term "common man" to imply "stupid," uneducated, lacking in sophistication, and easily controlled or manipulated. They look down on simplicity and believe themselves to be superior due to their material possessions. However, they fail to see that despite their wealth, they are more anxious than those who are humble or have modest means, because they are eternally anxious (5).

On the other hand, "simple man" is a label assigned to a group of people who, whether ignorant or not, mind their own business and are unconcerned with material wealth or social status or resign themselves to the fact that they cannot have anything else than what they already have.

Masks involve us in false things, in false relationships. We also have fake conversations, it's not for nothing that most human communication is fake. We often turn to social media to cultivate fake relationships and friendships. I say false because often "virtual friends" remain unknown to us beyond the façade they present online, other than the truth or falsehood they let be seen on their pages. Additionally, many of us use "masks" online to conceal our identities or assume different personas, but the reasons for doing it belong to each of us.

Political parties and national leaders engage in treacherous games on the political stage for the many. Behind the scenes, they remove some of their masks and scheme to increase their own wealth, destroy other nations, another country and harm another part of humanity, all in the name of their own "happiness".

Masks conceal our true feelings and the habits we want to keep hidden. We often fear expressing our thoughts in fear of judgment or isolation, so we wear a metaphorical mask. Underneath, we collect the poison we pour it out on others, believing them to be weaker and, easier to be manipulated as we want.

However, there are beings in this world who do not wear masks: children and man's best friend, the dog. They don't hide their feelings or intentions. Therefore, they do not wear them and will not know how to wear them. The dog is a very good psychologist and knows the man from a distance, it does not hide his appreciation or desire to attack. Children, who have not yet been "educated" to play by society's rules, have not yet learned to wear masks. I remember the expression my child used when he saw a person for the first time. He simply exclaimed: "you have such cold eyes!"

Children do and say what they feel. A child turns his back on you even if you are his parent, smiles or laughs with you even if you are a stranger. He shouts when he feels the need, laughs and cries. He expresses his emotions until we start to "educate" him and tell him "It's not beautiful", "it's not good", and "you're embarrassing me". The child smiles, laughs or cries among strangers, while you, under a "smiling mask", taught to suppress your true feelings, boil like a pressure cooker.

A Society without masks

Many wear their mask or masks everywhere in society, regardless of where they are. Only thanks to that will they have the strength to interact with others they may not forgive or want in their lives... But they also take off their mask when they return home from work or meetings. At home, we show who we really are. Perhaps this is why the saying "nowhere is like home" exists; we feel free from the constraints we face in the outside world. However, suppressing our emotions and sometimes allowing ourselves to be carried away by dark thoughts during the day does not help anyone. The more we suppress the feelings, the more they will want to surface. Thus, sometimes we erupt like volcanoes of anger, and we take revenge on those we consider weaker, on those who do nothing to prevent us from being ourselves, our loved ones, and our family members. When we take off our masks, they become our "workhorse".

By removing the mask, we become ourselves again. We allow ourselves to be who and what we really are. We allow ourselves to express what we did not do at the right time.

If we could speak up without fear of reprimand, ostracism, condemnation, or dismissal, we would live in a society where we express our opinions openly. A society where we don't hate each other because of our differing opinions. A society where we can say "thank you", "sorry", or "forgive me" without the fear of being considered "good and stupid" or put on the wall and ridiculed for our personal opinions. It would be a society where we are encouraged to discover our inner guru, our inner potential without being coerced, because we are all born worthy.

I envision a society where we appreciate the rights we are born with, without being labelled as having "blue blood" or not. A society where everyone has equal rights and access to information, rather than being manipulated due to differences in knowledge and the power of money. A society where individuals are not swayed by the agendas of a select few, who may seek to manipulate the masses through political slogans and biased interpretations of religious texts for their own gain.

In a society without masks, people would accept and embrace their differences. They would support each other selflessly and communicate openly, without resorting to masks. Similar to the concept of "holiday attire" versus everyday clothes, we employ a similar approach with masks, presenting our "best face" to outsiders, especially those who may aid our social standing, and our true selves to others. Yet, the choice of living with or without a mask reflects our beliefs and shapes the reality we experience, moment by moment.

Free Thinking

Okakura Kakuzo once said, "Our mind is the canvas on which artists paint; their pigments are our emotions; their chiaroscuro, the light of joy, the shadow of sadness" (29).

The thoughts and emotions we harbour act as the colours that shape our minds, helping us either overcome obstacles or work to our advantage. Thoughts trapped in the prison of fear can dull the colours of life. Conversely, free thoughts do not confine themselves to false norms or follow patterns for the sake of conformity, of being part of the many.

When one speaks and acts according to the expectations of others, they impose limits on themselves. By conforming to others' ideas and feelings, they confine their minds within certain walls that don't belong to them. Looking within with honesty, there might be a desire to break free from this closed space, but fear holds you back – fear of judgment by others, fear of exclusion, and fear of not fitting in. It's a fear of fears. However, if one listens to the voice of their soul, they will hear it urging them to follow their own path and be true to themselves. This authenticity and self-contentment are conditions of happiness, as Arthur Schopenhauer said, "The most blessed mortal is he who is content with his inner wealth, expecting fewer external pleasures" (5).

Thinking freely means not being confined to patterns imposed upon you, whether by society or by individuals. It doesn't involve trying to think like certain gurus or masters. Patterns exist everywhere and at all levels of society. Politics, religion, the educational system, medical, legal, financial, and mass media all impose on you patterns in which and how to live, which promote limited thinking required by society and restricted many times by lies, lacks, and rights existing only on paper.

Thinking freely means that you know that every problem has a solution, and nothing is impossible for you. You understand that every problem can have even more ways to solve it, and if one doesn't work, it doesn't mean the problem doesn't have a solution, you just don't see it at the time. Without getting attached to a particular way of solving the problem, to a particular solution, most of the time the solution that is offered to us is better than anything we previously imagined. Moreover, as a rule, it is "under our noses".

Additionally, it involves recognizing that each cell of our body has a vibrational frequency, an energy field, and the energy particles act as a whole. Thus, the body is based on an energy field that resonates with a certain frequency of vibration. In stressful conditions, this frequency is reduced and the body is under pressure. Thoughts trigger a stress response, we generate the emotion that vibrates with that thought, and we will experience anxiety, insecurity, and anger,... The thought that you are a victim will bring people and events into your life path that resonate on the same frequency as your thoughts. What you will experience will confirm that you are a victim. The thought that you can't have money or that you don't deserve it will attract a lack of money or its loss. Negativity in you will not attract positivity.

In ancient times, it was believed that negative emotions are stored in the body and affect its functioning on an anatomical and emotional level. The body represented by the subconscious does not differentiate between how we respond emotionally to a life experience and an emotion it manufactures from our thoughts because, to the subconscious, there is no difference. Your brain is unaware of who you blame and criticise. It doesn't know who you wish harm on, and your body will take any emotion for granted. Take personally what you "think" you give to others. And we only have about 60,000 thoughts a day, and most of them are negative and run every day. What you think is what you attract, therefore it is our own thinking that makes us sick, or as Dr Darren Weissman said in the movie E-motion (43), emotions, traumas, and subconscious memories are at the root of all disease.

While the subconscious mind involves complex neural processes from different regions of the brain working together, the limbic system is located in a specific region of the brain. By working its neural networks in harmony with other brain structures, it can control emotion, motivation, olfaction, behaviour, memory formation, sleep (dreaming), appetite, sexual appetite, and other physiological and emotional functions. The limbic system is like a control centre for conscious and unconscious functions, where the amygdala plays a vital role in controlling emotional behaviours such as fear, anger and anxiety. The limbic system makes no difference between you and others. It does not know the past and the future, it takes whatever is given to it, because it does not experience any difference between giving and receiving. It triggers the physical response to emotions (eg fear) and without it, we would not be able to process memories and express our emotions, we would not have survival instincts. Damage to the limbic system is evident in conditions like Post-Traumatic Stress Disorder.

People can experience a negative emotional state when exposed to someone emanating hatred or fear due to limbic resonance. This occurs because fear has long waves and makes that person's negative state exceed ours, which can impact and infect others, leading to what is commonly termed "mood contagion" in Western psychology.

For everything that troubles and hurts us, we tend to seek solutions outside ourselves. We blame others, cry, and complain because we often prefer feeling like victims. The more our emotions are influenced by external factors, the less we manage to make them spring from within us. However, the solution is not found in anyone or anything outside of us.

While memories can deceive people, intuition does not. The solution has always been within us, meaning we need to change our vibrational frequency. Just like changing the frequency of the radio when you hear something you don't like, all you have to do with emotions is turn the knob and change the frequency of the vibration from fear to the frequency of the heart.

How can we do this? Take your mind inside yourself and confront the emotional baggage you've been carrying for years. Don't carry it with you for your entire life! Uncover these emotions, analyze and accept them, as acceptance is a crucial step in the healing process that will allow you to reclaim your power. Along the way, forgive everything and everyone you believe you need to. It's not easy, but it's not impossible either.

If our Universe is a particle from a superuniverse, as Dan Farcaș says (8), it means that we are a particle, a universe in miniature. Like the universe, we are boundless and immortal, as Patricia Cori (32) says because we are made of atoms, protons, electrons and the pattern of infinite consciousness. According to this pattern, our soul is the centre of our own universe, built from compassion and love, and changing our frequency is just "one click" away! The solution is with you and lies within you!

5. Soul Flowers

When ye as men can learn that nothing but progress of Soul can count in the end, then truly ye are free from all bondage.
The Emerald Tablets of Thoth the Atlantean (40)

One of the earliest lessons we learn in life is to be "good, loving, and honest," but our experiences in family, school, and everyday life often seem to contradict these values. We may end up resigning ourselves to the belief "this is life." That we really resign ourselves, saying that this is what you want, this is what you know, this is what is good for you, we often do it because we believe we have no other alternatives, that in this life the money and the "chair" you sit on matter .

But what about the soul? Essentially, we come into this world in a body that is merely the shell for our soul. So how can we be different and feel free?

According to Taoists, the paths of Heaven, Earth, and Man are interconnected. TAO represents regularity and harmony, and the "true man"or the superior man spoken of by Lao Tze embodies TAO in action (18). He conceals his own radiance to be in harmony with others' darkness. Motivated by love, he does not seek to flaunt his brilliance, expect rewards, or judge others. He expresses gratitude for everything that comes his way in life. He lives from the soul, embracing the richness of the garden of love and offering forgiveness, trust, respect, and responsibility to others who are willing to partake in the wisdom of his soul.

Such a man becomes, as Okakura Kakuzo says, 'reluctant, like one who crosses a stream in winter; hesitating as one who fears those around him; respectful, as a guest; trembling like ice that is about to melt; modest, like a piece of wood not yet carved; empty, like a valley; formless, like troubled waters.' (29).

This man decided to change and alter the frequency of his education and living, as he believed that only through this could he break free from the false societal norms and embrace the wealth of his inner garden.

Forgiveness

The teachings of those around us often influence our beliefs and behaviours. They inherit many of these ideas from their teachers, including the notion that **we must seek permission for everything.** *However, in wiser circles, it is believed that* **asking for forgiveness is a preferable approach.**

We often simply accept certain things because they resonate with us, even if we don't fully understand them. We may accept them simply because "that's the way it is" or "that's how it has been since the beginning of time."

Is it so? I believe that the world should be a place of happiness and joy, lived from the heart. Unfortunately, the reality is that the world often seems to be filled with depression, stress, anger, spite, and hate. We are taught to seek permission for our rights and even for the smallest details of our lives, as if we have stolen our own lives and don't have the right to live them freely. Furthermore, we are often conditioned to place certain prerequisites on forgiveness or being forgiven – "they are angry with you," "they don't love you anymore," "you'll no longer have..." if you don't comply. In these conditions, we are learning a distorted version of forgiveness.

I see true forgiveness as a delicate white flower, which we trample underfoot whenever we say "I can't forgive", "I've forgiven, but I haven't forgotten what they did to me" or "I forgave them, but...". We destroy the essence of forgiveness whenever we attach conditions to it.

Going far behind the lack of sincere forgiveness, we have been more or less forbidden to express our emotions. Expressions like "why are you laughing?", "what reason do you have to laugh?", "why are you crying?", "you can't cry because it's a shame, because you're a man" - I not only heard them, but I have used them. I mean, I was the kind of "serious man" demanded by society's false norms, the polar opposite of my child who is a cheerful being, able to find fun in anything. Speaking of the Romanian, he likes to make caterinca.

*Forbidden laughter means the expression of seriousness and features the selfishness and false norms of society. For the world of love, laughter is an emotion that not only expresses itself, but is known to raise the vibrational frequency of those around us. It is the expression of joy, **"the ringing currency of happiness, our immediate gain"** says Schopenhauer (5).*

Laughter is the most powerful example of "mood contagion". Don't you also laugh when others laugh around you? Do you not feel present with those you laugh with? Isn't it for the same reason that we like to make the little ones laugh? In addition, laughter is a way of healing our body, which was very well explained after being experienced and used by Norman Cousins (28). But like anything else, it's healthy where it's used because there's something to laugh about. Using "laughter" to avoid feeling the pain hidden along with the traumas experienced does us no good.

Just as we can laugh freely because we feel good and express it, we can cry to externalize our pain, suffering, and we can do it regardless of whether we are a woman or a man, a child or an adult - to express our emotions.

We have the right to cry when we fall because there is no shame in doing so, just as there is no shame in making mistakes. But it is our decision whether we pick ourselves up and continue on our way or prefer to live in the valley of lamentation and pain as Irvin D. Yalom (14) says, unconsciously passing by what Alice Miller calls "our gold mines". (1)

Forgiving yourself and forgiving others means allowing yourself to feel without resorting to the weapons of fear, and without being afraid to be who you are. It means increasing self-esteem and self-love. By changing, you will see this change reflected in the attitude of others around you, and you will learn that forgiving is something natural that comes from within. It is an act of kindness to ourselves and to others.

Unconsciously, we don't forgive ourselves for not doing what we want, for not saying what we feel, for not taking a stand when our soul prompts. Instead, we accept what others want, and say, and follow them for fear of being isolated or cast aside. We don't forgive ourselves for many things in life and we don't do it because the lack of value and the idea that we are "weak" lives in us. When you look to your ego to hunt down mistakes, attached to hatred and malice, you remain attached to the past, return to anxiety and depression, and continue to live in the prison of fear. When you fall, feeling like a victim, you seek the support of selfishness to find the culprits around you, or you seek and offer false forgiveness also born out of fear.

Forgiveness needs to come from within us because it is a part of us and thus contributes to our personal growth. By forgiving ourselves, we can easily forgive others. We come to understand that everyone acts based on what they know, can, or want to do; everyone has the right to make their own choices. Learning to set our own limits is important, not because it upsets us, but because it is our right as human beings to define our personal space.

We are often taught to forgive with conditions, saying things like "I forgive you if..." or "I forgave you because...". This attitude seems normal, much like the laws set by those who commit wrongdoing in our world. However, such punishments come from a place of selfishness. In a world guided by love, even those we label as "criminals" are forgiven. If we were truly honest with ourselves, we would see how many times we have wished ill on someone due to our own inner suffering. This would help us understand the pain that those "criminals" carry within them, pain that they project onto others until their lives end. Punishing them does not necessarily lead to improvement; rather, it can result in increased frustration and hatred. The ease with which we dole out punishments to others reflects our own lack of forgiveness.

Conditional forgiveness is a false forgiveness given out of fear of the repercussions we might face in this life or the next. This is also a common teaching in churches. However, a god who forgives and loves with conditions is not a true and selfless god. A loving god does not punish because wrongdoing leads to learning lessons, and forgiveness itself exists within in the garden of love.

Conditional forgiveness is a form of forgiveness based on fear that can lead to repeatedly experiencing the same negative situations stored in your subconscious. Despite not wanting to relive these experiences, they resurface in different contexts with different people.

Unforgiveness stems from a lack of understanding and refusal to acknowledge mistakes. It hinders the attraction of positive things into our lives, creating an obstacle to happiness. Our inability to forgive is often rooted in punishment and a refusal to accept others' truths. This lack of forgiveness originates from the belief that others are superior or worthier than us, based on certain criteria we have been taught to judge worth by. However, everyone holds inherent value, regardless of qualifications, education, or wealth. No one is inherently superior or inferior. We all are born worthy.

In today's society, there is an apprehension towards displaying kindness to others. When acts of kindness are received, suspicions arise about underlying motivations, often encapsulated in the notion that "a good man is a fool." Despite this, kindness is a natural part of human nature.

The reluctance to embrace kindness is fuelled by subconscious feelings of inadequacy and unworthiness. This fear leads us to believe that we will become dependent on others or be taken advantage of, under the assumption "no good deed goes unpunished." However, kindness is present in children, who readily offer support and comfort to one another. As adults, we tend to withhold kindness and suspect others' intentions. We evaluate it and measure it. But kindness cannot be replaced by anything from the outside. To paraphrase C.S. Lewis (7), it is something that is needed in our world, and no outside law can take its place. Kindness comes from the heart, as an expression of love, and it has neither measure nor scale of evaluation.

Returning to forgiveness, a "real man" can easily overlook the words or actions that used to bother him because he has learned that everyone acts based on what they know, what they can do, and what they want. They cannot be changed by anyone outside. It is their right to change and it is their choice to do so.

Asking for forgiveness allows us to heal ourselves and others from inner pain. It helps us to let go of the weight of the past that we carry, and which builds up over time. Forgiveness becomes the path to physical and emotional healing. Through forgiveness, we learn to love, and restore broken relationships with our parents, siblings, or children, relationships that were damaged by hurtful words or actions directed towards us, not knowing that its freedom depends on our inner traumas. Life teaches us that the more we forgive, the better, calmer, and happier we feel. However, no one can offer full forgiveness for you, because no one can feel what you feel or how you feel, but yourself.

By forgiving myself, I learned to admit that I was selfish, because true forgiveness does not exist within the realm of selfishness. In doing so, I experienced what those I worked with later told me about clearing negative emotions, "I feel much lighter". True forgiveness leads to breaking and dissolving ties to past events we carry with us for years or even a lifetime, like tin cans tied to the car of newlyweds. The absence of forgiveness harms our health, while its presence gives us the gift and miracle of our body's ability to heal itself.

By resolving the memories of your past with kindness and forgiveness, you can get rid of the burdens you've been carrying. Some people start by forgiving others before forgiving themselves, while others do it in reverse. Regardless of the order, through forgiveness, we find our worth within ourselves and others. It helps us understand that whatever happened in our past, we were the best version of ourselves at that time, and it led us to where we are now. The past truly becomes history. Looking back, we can smile, understanding how liberating it is to live "free", unburdened by the weight of unforgiveness.

Our inability to forgive or our stubbornness to do it often stems from a lack of self-love. How can we love others when we can't love ourselves? True forgiveness requires no excuses, forgetfulness, or trust. It is the pure expression of the heart, that blooms without limits because it is part of the garden of love.

The events of recent years have brought us to the position of hating each other for various reasons or thinking about what we will do in case of war. Paganini says "The disorder produced in the application of the rhythm of history gives birth to storm and disturbance, lack of harmony in human society, just like the tuning fork that, wrongly fixed, scatters the powder of lycopodium on a blade." (4) Chinese wisdom teaches us that the greatest disharmony in man is disharmony between people. According to the teachings of the Yellow Emperor's Inner Canon, hatred makes one its slave, and when you hate someone, hatred hurts the heart that governs the blood vessels. We hurt ourselves and we don't know why we get sick.

War and poverty are created by us in the same way that tranquility, peace, and goodness are created. Every thought and emotion of ours goes out into the universe and adds to the evil or good already existing. Fear and hatred support them. Everything bad and negative directed at others, we direct at ourselves because, as I said, our limbic system does not differentiate between us and others. It takes for granted everything that is offered to it. The hatred and malice we direct at others is directed at us. Do we still wonder why the world is the way it is today? Every act of violence directed at others is first directed at ourselves. Hatred of others is hate directed at us or, as David Icke says (9), the real problem of the world we live in is ourselves.

In every moment of life you act as the best version of you. By forgiving yourself, you can truly forgive others. Looking for reasons to forgive, the act of forgiveness becomes false, because it is based on reasons, limits, and conditioning. Any mistake is punished and still gradually, with warnings, reductions in reward or lack of it. When you breathe in the pure fragrance of forgiveness, it will not look for reasons to give it.

Forgiveness brings about our change, which means letting go of resentment toward ourselves and others for what we believe wrongs. Using it, you will free yourself from those negative energies that increase pride, spite, arrogance, so that you don't rebuild the same situations that you actually don't like to live. It means accepting our shadow without seeking to project it onto others, channeling our own energy to become a better version of ourselves. Forgiveness is the key to the gate of the soul, beyond which we find everything we want and run after thinking we might never have: peace and happiness.

Like a flower that grows in the garden of love, forgiveness is prevented from coming to light by all the weeds that grow in the garden of selfishness and that attack it and can crush it so that it is not offered to anyone, conditioning it for the benefit of selfishness. However, it is within us and knows no fear. It is divine because it is the gateway to deliver the soul from all the weight we have thrown upon it. It is part of the richness of the soul.

Respect

Once we choose the path of forgiveness, we discover genuine self-respect and self-love.

We often claim to respect each other, but our actions may not reflect this. Despite our inclination to use words and slogans to assert our respect, our actions are the true indicators of our beliefs. However, respect exists within us as does forgiveness, but the education we receive often undermines both respect and forgiveness. Consequently, neither the advice we receive nor the "educational" measures imposed upon us will help us foster self-respect. To truly cultivate respect for ourselves, we need to face our childhood traumas and recognize the "weapons", the coping mechanisms we developed to protect ourselves. This process is essential for healing and rebuilding self-respect.

I would like to share a memory of my son with you. When I became a mother, I had to live with him at my parents' house for quite some time. Their home was in a suburb of the city, so it was common for music to be played loudly in some apartments. It didn't matter what kind of music was playing; whenever my child was and heard it, he would start dancing. People who poked their heads out of the window to look at him didn't matter, nor did those who laughed at him. For him, there was only the music and the joy of moving to its rhythm. Even at not even two years, my child loved (and still loves) music and the freedom to move as he pleased. (46)

I see this as an example of the self-respect that we are born with. Looking in dictionaries, respect is often defined as a feeling of admiration for someone or something, caused by their abilities, qualities or achievements. As parents, it is our responsibility to fulfil our children's needs, providing them with protection and respect. Unfortunately, in a world where many people didn't experience the moment of love in their childhood, that is, 90% of the world's population, as Alice Miller (2) says, experienced parental cruelty, we live with a distorted understanding of self-respect and respect for others. This can lead to resorting to violence, which stems from what we know, the negative experiences stored within us.

Where has our respect for the inner child gone? Where did we lose it? Where did we lost ourselves? In order to show true respect to others, we must first feel it for ourselves. You can't give something you don't feel you have, especially after experiencing emotional manipulation and the erosion of your sense of dignity through various forms of (parental) power dynamics (2).

I recall another memory from my life about ten years ago, after I left my position as a psychologist at the Directorate. I ran into an old acquaintance from my days as a teacher, who asked me directly, "Do you still work at the Directorate?" The forced smile that accompanied his question vanished when I answered, "No." She turned away and began looking at the shelves, seemingly preoccupied with everything she saw, without saying anything.

To me, it's an example of the artificial world we live in. We seem to think that respect is reserved only for those who are "great", meaning important and worthy according to the rational mind, and is a false respect built for our external world. It is bestowed upon us by our positions and wealth, and we in turn come to identify with that false value. It gives us the illusion that the rest of us also become significant if we associate with "important" people. Thus, respect for someone increases or decreases in direct proportion to the importance of their job, the size of their house, the number of cars in their driveway, and their bank accounts. We treat each other as if only some deserve respect, because we are taught that we cannot be respected unless we have a lot of money, houses, cars, and high ranked jobs.

The phrases "I want respect", "they don't respect me", and "you have to respect me" indicate the frustration of the person using them, feeling that they are not being respected. However, seeking respect from others may not address the underlying issue. If you respect yourself, why seek validation from others? What significance does others' respect hold for you? Have you considered that seeking respect from others may indicate a lack of self-respect?

In interactions with certain individuals in authority, one may perceive an air of condescension in their tone, something like "do you know who I am?" This illustrates how we can condition respect in a disingenuous manner. In doing so, we fail to genuinely respect one another. When respect is contingent upon one's social standing, it reflects a lack of self-worth. We extend politeness or so-called respect to individuals of certain standing, while being rude to those in lower-ranking positions. This behaviour reflects a lack of respect for ourselves.

Lack of self-respect is also evident when remaining in a job out of fear of not finding a better one or believing that one is not capable of pursuing a different career path.

Self-respect gained through money or any other forms stemming from societal conditioning is not genuine. It is a form of selfishness. When you strive to be like someone else, you are dwelling in your own insecurities and lack of self-respect. You begin living in a lie, telling lies to yourself, and becoming comfortable with this falsehood, which is just a small part of the big lie we live in.

The more you seek validation from others, the more diminished and unworthy you feel in their presence. Similarly, when you expect someone else to meet your standards, it is a reflection of your own feelings of inadequacy. In reality, it is you who feels inadequate because deep down, you do not believe you deserve respect. Driven by these negative thoughts, you will do anything to gain respect from those around you.

Furthermore, when you harbour hatred towards those with differing religious or sexual orientations, you are hating a part of humanity. Each of us is a unique aspect of humanity and we all have the same right as you to choose how to live our lives. Your lack of self-respect leads you to disregard the right of others to live as they choose. You're the one who doesn't respect yourself enough, then, as a Romanian expression says: why would I be worried about the "neighbour's goat"?

Treating every person with the same level of respect, without giving in to the comparisons offered by your mind such as "he's poor", "he's uneducated", "he's unattractive", "he's the boss of...", "he's the teacher...", "he's homosexual", is the true mark of respecting oneself and others. Embracing Albert Einstein's words, "I speak to everyone in the same way, regardless of whether he is the clerk or the president of the university" (44) as a guiding principle in your daily life will ensure that you respect not only yourself but also everyone else.

On the other hand, when you haphazardly leave your trash behind or throw it in a bush or river, you are not respecting nature. In a way, you also contribute to the lack of respect for nature. Polluted waters full of garbage, entire deforested forests show little or no respect from us. Think about everything you buy, how much you buy, what you consume, and how much you consume. Perhaps then you will understand how disrespectful you are to yourself, to others, and to the planet. Why are you surprised by natural calamities?

Confucius says, "Respect yourself, and others will respect you" (44). Lise Bourbeau considers respect one of the three necessities for the well-being of our mental body, along with truth and sincerity (20). She also says that they help us avoid respiratory ailments, allergies, and problems in the throat. When I first read her book, the information made sense to me. I had lived too long hiding from others' truths and my own fears. My body was always suffering from respiratory ailments and allergies. It took a few more years before I understood where I needed to look for their causes. To understand that I had to search in the traumas stored in my subconscious and listen to my body to regain my self-respect.

Real respect is not the feeling we have towards someone because of their possessions, achievements, or status. It doesn't come from comparing ourselves to others. Respect comes from within, from being proud of who you are as a person. When you respect yourself, you also respect others simply because they are human. Thus, you see that respect is not about measurement or comparison. It means setting your own personal boundaries, believing in your truth, and standing up for what you believe in.

In the society where everything is evaluated, nothing is respected. When we respect, we don't judge because we understand the role of differences in the beauty of this world and that the value is within you and me and each of us. Seeing each other as another facet of being human is true respect. It is intrinsic and cannot be bought or sold; it is part of the foundation of love and simply exists.

RESPECT YOURSELF in order to earn respect from others!

Truth

As I have already said, respect exists within us and becomes evident when we encounter different opinions. In any discussion, someone not only has a different opinion, but as a rule of our society, we seek debate not for the sake of understanding multiple perspectives, but rather out of a selfish desire to prove our superiority in front of someone, to earn our "respect".

Being different, it is natural to have different opinions, because they stem from our individual truths, or as Neville Goddard (27) says, "Two men looked from behind bars; one saw the tin, the other saw the stars."

Which of the two is right? Whose side is the truth? Each of the two has the same view in front of them and, yet, they perceive differently. Scientifically, the notions based on which we define our statements have only a relative character, ie they depend on the "position of the observer", as Fritoj Kapra says (12). Psychologically, our unique perceptions shape our individual truths. From any position, everyone's truth is completely different, because no one holds the monopoly of truth as W. W. Atkinson stayed (38). Being unique, each of us possesses a unique truth based on our intuition and convictions.

I used to say what I thought, but I was criticised and ridiculed by many who knew me. I cried because it hurt, but I didn't know at the time that it wasn't their attitude that hurt me, but my lack of knowledge of my inner self and my own convictions that made me feel the pain.

It does not mean that I have always been fair to myself and stood up for my own truth. I avoided saying many things in the idea of not hurting myself or hurting others. In reality, in both cases, I was lying to myself, because the pain was only mine. It came from everything I had experienced as a child. On the one hand, because being too young I didn't know what was happening, what was my fault for what I was experiencing, and then because my truth, lived by me and seen with my physical eyes, was forbidden to be my truth. All those avoidances of speaking in order not to upset, not to disturb, not to be put aside, caused me many ailments, but this is not the place to talk about them.

However, we don't want to feel pain because we don't like the taste of it. Nevertheless, why does the truth told by others hurt us so much? Ultimately, everyone has their own truth, and the lessons that are served to us through other people are all for our own good.

As humans, we have many expectations from others and ourselves. We expect to be respected and believed. But where you don't give to yourself and others, do you want to receive? Do you want to receive something that you do not give? You can't just do one of two. Every coin has two sides. "Everything is double, everything has two poles, everything has two extremes", says the teaching of the Kybalion (39).

Our inner truth is inside us and wants to come out, but it is often suppressed. Many times it tries to break free and we suffocate it. We don't give it the chance to be free, not knowing that we don't allow ourselves to be honest with ourselves and feel truly free. Where the real pain begins and hangs in us, we didn't know and weren't helped to understand what was happening. Rationally, we know that our own truth is punished because it is not in agreement with the truth of the "greater" than us. But beyond reason, I didn't know why I should be punished when telling my truth. That is why many times, we do not speak our own truth in life. We worry about the reaction of others or what the consequences will be for us, even though every action has consequences. Respecting ourselves, we assume them. Just wanting to "play" a piece within the limits of safety, we don't give ourselves respect. Why? Because in the first place, there is no such thing as safety that lasts as long as we live. It is a lever used by selfishness to ensure its "power". However, by embracing our truth, we can let go of our inner baggage and feel more confident. You love yourself!

Furthermore, those who refuse to accept your truth are being selfish, too. Unconsciously, they want you to conform to their way of thinking. It can be challenging for many people who live within society's norms to comprehend a different perspective. As a response, we may feel the need to prove our truth is better, undermining their self-confidence through selfish tactics.

Speaking your truth means not hiding or having to remember that you said something else than what you felt at that moment. It means being fair to yourself and showing self-respect. You don't lie to others because you don't want to lie to yourself and you don't like being lied to either - this aligns with the teaching "treat others as you would like to be treated".

For generations, we have been living by the same rules, such as the "watch what you say" guideline, created and upheld by those seeking "importance". In a society where everything appears to be regulated and needs approval, what can be a solution? When everything seems to be measured and dictated by those in authority, where do we turn?

I turn to the quiver of memories again, and again to the time when I was a student at the Pedagogical High School. I vividly recall overhearing a heated discussion between my parents one day after returning home from classes. My father was a principled and straightforward man, who detested flattery and arrogance. On that particular day, he was furious as he explained to my mother that he had been warned by the local president of the Romanian Communist Party to refrain from speaking out, otherwise risking his daughter's expulsion from high school. This warning stemmed from my father's outspokenness at party meetings, where he, a simple worker, fearlessly voiced his opinions about the working and living conditions of himself and his colleagues. He dared to be himself in front of the "big ones". (46)

Does the scenario sound familiar? The same kind of scenario is happening now. Well, yes, it's different because now I'm also over forty years older.

A similar version to the one narrated above, I lived while working as a psychologist at the Directorate. I vividly remember being alone in the office when my boss walked in and handed me a file, instructing me to handle it. I knew from other colleagues that she had this habit, it was her usual modus operandi, and as with everything, the beginning is the hardest. Once you have taken the first step, you become entangled in the "mafia". You entered the choir, you played...

I didn't have any issue with the file that was given to me. For me it was another file, another destiny. The problem came when I opened it and I seen that there were no supporting documents for the disease my boss claimed the person had, and for which she had brought the file for me to fill out. I told her that I was preparing the sheet that was requested, filled in with the person's data, and that was it. She continues: "you fill in what you have to write as a psychologist and sign. I will add the documents later when I have them". I refused to do so. I explained to my boss that as a psychologist, when I write something, I am also taking responsibility for it by signing it. I didn't want to just do what someone else wanted me to do, especially if it compromised my professional integrity. In addition, I did not rub my elbows on the bench learning to be in a position to do what another wants, just because that one is hierarchically superior. The boss was fuming, but kept quiet. What came next? Stupefaction!? She took the file with the information I had filled out while we were talking and threw it in the trash.

Consequence? As I have said on other occasions, I had previously confronted others who were hierarchically higher in the institution, so I did no longer met the requirements to apply again for that job.

By standing up for your own truth, you are often punished in various ways. Understanding that you have also accepted the consequences of your actions, you have no reason to complain. So, I told my truth and suffered the consequences. I understood that my time in that institution was over because I refused to be manipulated or controlled by others. By telling myself the truth, I no longer accepted being anyone's puppet.

Sometimes we acknowledge the truth, sometimes we suppress it with tears. But there are also times when we are scared of what we might reveal. These days, we stay silent because we fear losing our jobs and money.

How often do you speak your mind? If you don't, you're only suppressing yourself, and this can lead to inner turmoil and physical illness. I was once told by a colleague how much they admired my courage. Is it truly brave to express your thoughts and feelings? Or is it considered courageous simply because society tries to silence us with rules and punishments? Is it forbidden to speak our truth just because someone holds a prestigious title or degree? They also have a head, body and legs just like you, and the title is not glued to the forehead, nor is the seat to the... back. We all have the right to express our thoughts, opinions, and truths, and we can all decide if we do or not. Other people's power is just an illusion, and we are the ones who feed it because we are the ones who give power to others by not speaking our truth.

Where is my freedom when I am punished for what I say and do even when I'm not hurting anyone? I've felt like a puppet, saying and doing what others want for years. I felt like I was in a puppet show, where others pulled the strings. I won't say things only to make others comfortable because I believe "What you think about me is none of my business" (36). Moreover, if I disagree with you, it won't be because I don't respect your opinion, but because I have my own truth and I don't accept being at the mercy of your strings. In all honesty, I'll always be true to myself.

If we analyze the truth through the lens of couples when relationships break down, it's common for each person to blame the other for their misery instead of seeing their own faults. They search through the pile of miseries they believe they have experienced, but only one culprit, he for her and she for him. Although, this it is not always the case, as things can happen differently...

In the most common scenario, each person involved in the relationship tends to focus only on the good things they did themselves and ignore the other part's contribution. As if the relationship is only about what was bad in the relationship. Everyone's selfishness wants to prove how good they are or they are superior to the other. By this demonstration made, one of them bears no blame, for it rests entirely on the other. They are so fierce in fighting their selfishness that they don't give themselves credit for all the beautiful things they experienced in their relationship, as if the relationship itself was just a continuous failure. However, just like in a tango, a successful relationship requires both parties to play their part and stay true to themselves while maintaining harmony. The situation worsens when the families of the individuals become involved in their relationship or its dissolution.

Apart from visible signs of physical violence, there are often invisible emotional and psychological scars left by the relationship, known only to the person who bears them. Sometimes, they are not aware of the each other's pain. No one knows them except the person who bears the wounds. Then you can say that your truth is also the other's?

Each person tends to see the relationship only through the lens of their own perspective, driven by their own selfishness. What would it be like to allow ourselves to see the world the way we want to see it? What would it be like to understand others by trying to put ourselves in their shoes and, to paraphrase Irvin D. Yalom (14), see the world as they see it? How would it be not only to speak our own truth, but also to hear another's, because, as Napoleon Savescu says, "there is a DESTINY OF THE TRUTH, and it only needs two groups of people to come out to revelation: some to SPEAK it and... others to HEAR it... !" (24).

Take a moment to observe the trees and flowers around you. Each one is bathed in the same light, yet they follow their own unique path, respecting the truth of others. An olive seed will only grow into an olive tree, just as a crocus bulb will only bloom into a beautiful flower. It's important not to live within the boundaries and decisions of others if you want to be truly free. Freedom comes from discovering your own truth and respecting yourself for who you are.

Embracing your truth allows you to accept that others have their own truths as well.

Never hesitate to speak your truth. If you don't stand up for yourself, no one else will. Remember the words from the Emerald Tablets of Thoth the Atlantean (40): "Do not be silent when evil is spoken, for the Truth, like the rays of the sun, illuminates everything." Speak your truth because it leads to true freedom and also allows others to do the same. As Napoleaon Savescu said, "No Religion or Law above the truth." (24)

Sincerity

Truth goes hand in hand with sincerity. We experience it fully, in its purest form, as children, and then again when we have children of our own. This sincerity is the expression of our inner harmony. Where did we lose it? Why are we afraid of it?

Years ago, I came across an expression that stuck in my mind: "water is water, and tea is tea." You might say, "Well, obviously," but the deeper meaning behind these words led me to a new understanding. Moreover, most of us have likely tried tea at least once in our lives or are aware of its beneficial effects on health - regular consumption strengthens the body. However, what does tea have to do with sincerity?

The essence of the tea ceremony lies at the heart of tea culture, embodying harmony, peace, sincerity, and happiness. In Japanese culture, the tea ceremony is a profound event where spiritual training is of utmost importance. It takes place in a special room and is considered "an improvised drama woven from tea, flowers, and paintings," as described by Okakura Kakuzo. where there is "No colour to disturb the tone of the room, no sound to spoil the rhythm of things, no gesture to destroy the harmony, no word to disturb the unity of the scene, all movements to be executed simply and naturally." (29) This commitment to harmony is at the core of the tea ceremony.

Each stage of the process employs a different technique, from preparing the tea equipment to drinking the tea. Every cup of tea represents the harmony between water and fire, each with its own story. Furthermore, each cup of tea is a symbol of pure beauty, and according to Sotumpa, purity holds the same power as a virtuous person. The tea ceremony **embodies respect, purity, and tranquility, with harmony as its essence**. *The most crucial aspect is to have a pure heart and to seek* **sincerity**. *(29)*

Harmony is essential for all of us, but where can we find sincerity? It is always present in the eyes of a child who looks at you with all the love they have, or in the eyes of man's best friend - the dog - who waits for you for hours or days, never doubting for a moment that you will not return to them. There is no need to search far and wide for it, as sincerity, like respect, resides within us.

Often, when I was criticised for being too honest because no one supposedly deserves it, I questioned myself, "Is honesty something that exists to be appreciated? Is my worth as a human being determined by how I handle the feelings of others? Am I nobody because I'm honest? Are you nobody if you show honesty or receive it from someone else? We are all born worthy, and each of us seeks sincerity from those around us. So, what reason is there not to be truthful with ourselves and others? The response to the last question was that people suffer from honesty.

They are true words, when you live selfishly. I had to endure a lot of suffering for many years until I understood the cause behind them, especially when I was told that I was "too honest" and lacking "diplomacy". I admit that I didn't know and if I tried it was poorly used. For me, diplomacy means wearing a mask and using it you can be fake for personal gain from those with whom you maintain those "diplomatic relations". Therefore, the thought of being diplomatic made me anxious about the potential consequences of my words and actions. It was causing me a lot of pain.

*To avoid suffering we prefer to run away from honesty and truth, resorting to lies instead. Suffering makes us feel weak and worthless. We make the lie a part of our existence, and the pain we feel is similar to not accepting that we prefer to be lied to. While we appreciate honesty from others, deep down, we may unconsciously prefer to be lied to as we believe lies cause less pain than the truth. It's just that **"A repeated lie becomes a truth and a neglected truth passes into the occult space".** (24)*

Lies are present in every stratum of society, at every level, and it also cause turmoil within families. Thus, the man hides things, and facts from his partner, in the idea that he will avoid a fight or an agreement, but he does it out of fear, for reasons hidden inside him, unknown or unwanted to be known for fear of pain.

The child who hides something or lies does it for the same reasons, where we can also add his desire to be "seen and listened to" by adults. They look for the attention or moment of love that is delayed. However, children are the most sincere beings. They are the pure expression of simplicity and innocence, pure love.

Adults, already attached to the pattern in which they were educated, avoid honesty on the grounds of not suffering. Yet, no matter how much you hide and postpone the moment of honesty, it will still come, and you will pay a price directly proportional to the time spent in lies or false assumptions. To be honest, you will be judged bitterly by our selfish society, and you will be in the position of choosing...

I am reminded of the "Defamation of Paganini", and his attitude towards the lessons in which he took care of his students carefully and at length, versus the attitude he had towards King George IV who invited the violinist to perform at Windsor Castle for a pittance. Paganini declined the sovereign's invitation by suggesting that he should buy a seat in a row on the ground floor of the opera house in London because it would cost him less. His sincerity was condemned by many people of the time who considered him arrogant because he dared to offend the king.(4) Cowardice did not allow them to see the violinist's sincerity which came from trust in him and in the music he offered to the world, regardless of who was listening to it.

Suppressed by ridicule, sincerity often becomes more and more difficult to express towards certain people, and certain situations and thus, it diminishes within our soul. We hide it out of fear, under shame, guilt, and all that inner baggage we carry inside us. As we become more reluctant to be honest with others, we lie more and more to ourselves. We avoid anything that we think can suppress our confidence, question every person we encounter, and build on the negative emotions we already have within us.

According to Lao Tze, "In the heart of man virtue is the beatific void." In beneficence, virtue is the charm of mankind. In speech there is sincerity. In administration, there is good leadership. In activity, is the performing power. In action is the time, the ruin, the most favourable moment. Virtue alone works and fights, so it does not make enemies." (18).

Sincerity brings peace of mind, when using it towards ourselves or others, allowing us to rest well. Then why not live with it? "Morality" is instilled in us, but we are born with integrity.

Faith

We cry and complain, laugh and smile... We live our lives based on what we know, want, or are able to do. We don't know how long our lives will be, but regardless of our age, theoretically, we all know it's too short not to enjoy it.

Because we are not perfect, we are taught that we "must" do a lot of things to achieve, in a way, perfection. A chimaera that can become like a lifelong race. However, death will meet us as we are still "imperfect". It's just that we are all born worthy and that's why I often say that we are all perfect in what is called our "imperfection".

Additionally, because it is a "must", we learn what others offer us as knowledge and believe mostly what is seen with the physical eye, even though everything seen with the physical eye was first originated from the unseen. It stems from a person's belief in themselves and their power. Whether or not we believe we are born worthy is up to us. Therefore, we act in virtue of it or lament and grieve over our lives a lot.

Many times we say "I no longer trust...". This lack of trust is based on the same lack of self-worth that I have been mentioning, which also attracts a lack of trust in us. We do not believe in ourselves, because unconsciously, we are not worthy and are weak. Thus, the education we receive, and the influence of society make us look for our value externally. The people around us are only our mirror, of our thoughts and emotions, or as C. Jung says, "Everything that irritates us in others helps us to discover ourselves" (44). What we dislike in others is often a reflection of our own traits, but selfishness is considered above everything and everyone. Each of us sees our own mistakes, habits, and defects mirrored in others, but our reaction is often, as Schopenhauer says, of "the dog that, looking at itself in the mirror, barks without knowing that it is paying attention to its own image."(5)

Our lack of trust in ourselves leads us to seek confirmation, appreciation, and full confidence in the words or actions of others *without valuing our own, or sometimes we discard them because we believe they have no worth. The same lack of trust leads us to believe that someone else, a person or entity, is the one to trust. Something that belongs to you from birth you give up and expect others to give it back to you. It's just that no one owes you to give you your self-confidence or restore for you what you consider to have been lost. Your thoughts belong to you. Is there any point in blaming someone else?*

Expressions like "I believed in vain, it was not fulfilled" or "I don't believe until I see" denote a lack of faith, and you can't just have "little faith," because as Lao Tze said, "Having only 'little faith' means "not having faith". (18) Faith, like everything else, knows units of measurement only in the world of selfishness, and is evaluated according to our negative thoughts and emotions that remain prisoners within us.

Confidence exists within us, in our own power. Just as you believe that the flower seeds you plant in your garden will grow into the flowers you desire or imagine, you need to believe in yourself and what you want from your life. Think about it, how do you live it? How do you want to live it?

The belief that comes from fear is the basis of the control and manipulation exercised over us by the "big ones" and those who make the games behind the scenes. The faith that comes from our soul only exists, in the love that is within us, just as there is truth, sincerity and respect.

I was saying in another chapter that the subconscious defines us. Living by the rules set by the selfish mind, our beliefs will define our reality in a way that we dislike, but we adapt to it and let it become the comfort in which we live our lives. We live this way because we are afraid to try another facet of the information that reaches us, or we prefer the comfort in which we live and do not want to change anything.

The changes that come in our lives destroy the comfort that we like and that we are used to. But everything is a movement, an evolution, a continuous change, because "even the infinite fire that changes its colours is not the same from one day to the next" says Thoth the Atlantean (40). Seen through the lens of Taoism, change is an essential characteristic of nature, says Fritoj Kapra (12), and the laws of nature are not imposed from the outside. Everything comes from within.

Our change comes from within. Therefore, the more we resist these changes out of fear of them, the more unhappy we feel. However, the changes happen anyway. Today, we are no longer who we were yesterday, and our version of tomorrow will be a completely different one, better and wiser. We say that life only goes forward, so we move on, overcome obstacles and we can if we want, appreciate everything that life offers us. Why do we do it? Because there is trust, there is faith in us.

When you dream, you imagine something you want, and that dream can become reality. You are the only one who can decide whether to give it life or not, and only you do it by believing in yourself and your dream, in the power that exists within you and in your worth as a human being, because only you are YOU.

If we follow the thread of the element of faith through Buddhist doctrine, it says that our original state is that of Buddha, and to enter nirvana it is enough to believe strongly in this original state. We can liken this "Pure Land" as they call it, to the state of the child who, no matter how he occupies his time, is happy. Faith is at home in the child who draws, sings, plays and dances. Appreciated and encouraged, he will become an adult with self-confidence, confidence in his own strength, and a man who will believe in himself. Compared to others, scolded, and punished, will lead to the repression of suffering, and the repression will lead to "emotional blindness"(1). The child will also lose his trust, becoming an anxious adult and will constantly seek confirmation from something or someone around him. He will look for confidence externally.

We have a lot of synonyms for the word faith: trust, conviction, confidence, help, dependence... towards something or someone. It is defined as "strong trust or confidence in something or someone". Again something or someone that is outside of you? What about the power within you?

Expressions like "you don't do well because you don't have faith, because you don't believe in..." are true not because I don't follow your religion or someone else's. "We" are not doing well because this is our conviction, this is the belief by which we live: "that it is not going well for you". You convey to the universe that you are not good, that you need others or something else to believe in, and we will experience things that confirm our convictions.

Neville Goddard says "faith must be interwoven with understanding to acquire that active quality which it does not have by itself." (27) To have faith is to believe in the divine/ God that exists within you and every human being. If we do not believe we can, we don't have what we need, we don't believe in ourselves. If we don't do it, can we ask others to do it for us? ***We reflect ourselves in others, and the world is our mirror. It reflects back to us.*** *We cannot ask others what we do not even offer ourselves, because as C. S. Lewis says, "You can't know, you can only believe or not."(44)*

When we use the word "believe", it does not mean that I can see, hear, touch that thing that I believe in, but I simply know, I feel that it comes from within me. To believe only if I can use my senses, means that I condition my faith, turning my belief into a false one.

We often believe in what those around us, close or not, offer us. Some do it selflessly because they care about us, and love us in their own way. Others do it out of interest.

Selflessness is when you give love without conditions because by believing in yourself, you believe that others may also be able to pass that love on. You believe because you know you are born worthy. Loved ones can comfort you or fuel your fears because they don't accept you can change yourself. They are afraid of losing you, and at the same time, they live the fear that they are not doing anything to fulfil their dreams, only that they are not ready to change themselves because they fear what this change brings with it.

When you act out of true love, you believe and will not seek to impose your ideas, dreams or fears. You will respect everyone's own space, support them and where appropriate, you will be with that person because you believe in them and their wishes.

Others may support you with interest even if they don't believe in your dreams because the weeds of selfishness are in full bloom in their garden. Thus, their support will not stem from trust in you or your dreams and from the belief that you will do what you dream, but rather from vanity, cowardice, spite, hatred, desire for revenge, or false self-worth.

To have faith means I know everything is okay. *Following my intuition, true faith is in its message, in what I feel. Being part from the Source we all come from, it never tells us lies because it is truth, it is part of our consciousness and part of the universal consciousness. Therefore, do you need something or someone to believe in yourself? Believing only in someone else or something else, you live life according to the concepts formulated by others, without thinking about* *what you feel. Or if you do, you're afraid you're wrong, because that's what you've been taught from what you've lived. Making a mistake becomes a sin that must be punished in this life or after death, right?*

It is customary as having a certain religious faith, to blame those who do not have the same faith as yours. But how do you know that your belief is the true or correct one? Doesn't that religious belief you speak of, whatever it is, urge you to love your neighbour? Is your relative the only one of a religion with you? Then your religion is a selfish one because it divides. Do you blame and judge others for their faith? It means that your religious faith is also limited, it is conditional. A true faith does not judge or restrain anyone, nor does it punish.

By only accepting your own version, you are using your own limited beliefs and you don't want to go beyond them, to accept that others have different beliefs. You choose your truth as the absolute truth and thus choose to live selfishly. You cannot, do not know or perhaps do not want to see another facet of the truth in which we live. To understand that being unique, each person has their own truth because they have their own belief and value system.

*On the other hand, do you need **a guru** to have faith? Every guru or master you believe in is a person like any other, who has forged his own path. What he experienced brought him to where he is and made him who is. It doesn't mean that the path he took is the best or the least good for you. It is the best path for the one who has walked it. You cannot walk anyone's path but your own. Every person you meet on your path leaves an energetic imprint in one way or another on your path. You decide how much and how you use that fingerprint. You cannot copy it, because you are only YOU and you are the only guru you need to listen to.*

Your self-confidence does not need confirmation from others, because no one will know exactly what your dreams and desires are. No one can live your desires, your aspirations, but yourself. No one can change or resolve your traumas if you don't. Neither the money nor the idea that you "must" do it, will help you.

From what I experienced, I understand that "must", "need" and "money" are some points that are part of the circle of selfishness in which we revolve for years, and some, all our lives, living and reliving the same events. However, only we decide if and when we break through these walls of fear. It is not an easy path, but anyone can do it, because according to an axiom of the Kybalion, "no one escapes the principle of cause and effect", but any of us can use the laws of "the higher planes to master the laws of the lower planes." (39)

Liberation from the unseen walls of fear is the soul's liberation from worries, needs, pride, carelessness, and revenge. The garden of your life is truly revealed to you... You find the happiness that lives within you and you understand how important the moment NOW is because it is the only time you have.

Running to a job that others give you for what, when and how much they want, even if you don't like it or don't want it, is conditioning. It limits your time and often your health. You keep yourself in a prison, the one of fear that you will have no way to live. You are the one who locks your dreams or measures them, without counting your life can end at any moment. Measuring your dreams, and your desires is like giving an exact dimension to the universe.

Man's dreams should neither be measured nor evaluated. They are neither big nor small, neither worthless nor unimportant. Every dream has its boundless value to the one who has it. Those who think that they "didn't get enough time" to do what they want to do today or don't complete what they started, will someday experience the bitterness of their procrastination. Those who give more than they feel they can carry will experience bitterness in a different form. Either of these two options is extreme, they mean a lack of confidence in yourself and a lack of harmony, and they are also born from your lack of worth, from the idea that you are not good enough. In these conditions, we turn our life into a ship that is supported by suffering as oars, as Schopenhauer says (5).

Living life "dragging back and forth like a pendulum" (39) you are more unhappy, and unhappiness makes you look for so-called happiness externally rather than internally. You live in a world of short-lived illusions of earnings, believing that they will bring you happiness. From these illusions, some become addicted to substances, alcohol, and sex. However, no matter how much you drink or how long you use substances, not even how much you earn in your life, none of these options will free you from your inner pain. If we look at the Compendium of Materia Medica, excessive drinking will injure the mind, harm the blood, upset the stomach and weaken the strength of the spirit. Everything needs moderation. Excesses become excuses to run away from what hurts you and you delude yourself that you still found something to make you experience happiness. You can call them self-inflicted punishments that you apply to yourself because you are not good enough, you don't trust yourself, you don't think you can be a worthy person. I know the path of worthlessness that I have walked and I know how much suffering I have accumulated inside me.

As long as we live under the power of selfishness, our world is divided into "me" and the rest. That signifies, according to Hinduism, we are chained by karma. Freedom from selfishness and karma involves recognizing our interconnectedness with the whole, of oneness with nature and our actions following it. It means, says Fritoj

Kapra, experiencing the liberation experience called "moksha" which is the ultimate goal of Hindu philosophy. Following the Buddha's Third Truth, which involves eliminating suffering, we leave samsara, free ourselves from karma and reach the state of total liberation where "the conception of a separate self disappears and one experiences the constant sensation of the world as a whole, as a unity." (12)

We are taught to see everything with the mind's eye and to look outside ourselves for whatever we believe would bring us happiness. The soul does not need things built outside of itself to be truly happy, because it is rich in having everything it needs to be happy. You don't worry about what might happen or make mistakes. You are not afraid of the consequences because you know that everything that happens in your life has a reason and brings you lessons to learn. Giving up the fear of thinking differently, you can think "without limits", freely.

When your boss tells you "You don't know who you're talking to" or "You're fired" or "There's no money to pay you", he's doing everything he can with your time and your job because he thinks he has the power to control you. But his power is tied to a chair, a tag on the door, and the money poured into his bank. Take away his chair and his money, and he will be lesser than you. He will in turn only be his fears and frustrations, his pride and thirst for false power driven by his selfishness.

Perhaps you are afraid to talk to him, to tell him your opinion. Do you see him as a different being, not as you, when you talk to him? To believe in what you feel you have to do! Do not fear the consequences of speaking up. If you lose your job, you will look for another one or do something else than what you were doing. After you say what you feel like saying, you will feel freedom and relief. That's why we say "I freed myself", "I took a burden off my soul". Believe in yourself!

At the same time, no matter how many jobs you change, you can feel like you're not good enough or don't have enough. No matter how rich you are, you want more and more things and money, because "wealth is like salt water says Schopenhauer (5), the more you drink, the more thirsty you are". Regardless of the high position you are in, you want a higher position, you want more money, you want... There is nothing wrong with wanting and evolving. You hurt yourself and others when you are driven by selfishness. You carry all your pain around until you find the strength to go inside yourself, to change your belief system, to resolve and change everything that needs to be changed.

Think about it, if you knew that today was your last day on earth, what would you do? What would you change about yourself? Would you fulfil a dream or make more money? Would you seek to forgive, love more, or run after money?

In any change, it all begins with the desire to want and intend to be different. Before you begin to change, or according to TAO, change comes from within because the laws of change come from within the very things of this world (12). Only you feel that desire because it comes from within you. Only you can believe in your intuition and you don't need confirmation to follow it.

I also said that after working abroad for several years, I returned to the motherland. I listened to my intuition because I believed what I felt, regardless of the reprimands I received from most around me.

Several years ago, after leaving my last job, I decided to pursue another dream: buying an old house in a village, having a garden, planting whatever I want, working the land as I please, and sustaining myself directly from my work. Despite few people supporting my desire, I knew it was mine, and only I could take action to make it come true.

At the time, I lived in a neighbourhood on the edge of the city with a lot of filth and loud music in the closest blocks. Few people encouraged me to sell the flat. Most of those who heard about my desire to sell it told me that I would never give it away and advised me not to make hasty decisions. Many others had their flats for sale, some for years, and the area was not very sought after.

The sale did not happen in a month or even in half a year, but I did not despair. I believed I would sell it because I could envision myself staying at home and working in the garden. Consequently, I eventually sold the apartment and bought an old house. Some said that I was "lucky," but luck does not exist. Our "luck" is within us, shaped by our thoughts and emotions. I succeeded because I believed in my intuition and my dream.

No matter how many people you listen to, you can prove everyone right, but none of them will feel what you feel. What your heart tells you, it will not tell others, because only you are YOU. It's your belief in yourself that makes you see steps where others don't, and they don't because they don't believe. You don't even need someone else to believe in your dream. It belongs to you, it is your creation. It is your faith in yourself and your dream that prompts you to overcome your fears.

I am aware that any advice we receive comes from the perceptions and experiences of the person giving it. However, I can tell you that you can achieve anything you want, just let your heart be your guide. Listen to your inner voice and believe in it!

Kant teaches us that we should seek the world within ourselves, not outside of us (44). The mind may present many *obstacles, but the heart knows no barriers. It understands your path and believes that anything is possible, because faith means certainty. It is up to you to find your own faith. Don't be among those who leave this world unhappy because they didn't live their lives the way they wanted. Who do you think will be responsible? We can find many reasons and culprits, but the only one responsible for being unhappy and dying with regrets is you.*

To repeat what I said earlier, the soul knows no lack of trust, only the ego does. Trusting in yourself and your soul leads you to the best path in life, and only you can decide the path you want to follow. You are the only one who can decide whom to trust and have the power to live your life the way you want. You have the ability to decide whether or not to believe in yourself and your power, because "Man is only what he thinks he is, a brother of darkness or a child of Light" (40).

Courage

The lack of faith makes us live in a state of unhappiness, of insecurity, to be in a continuous search for something that will make us happy, and in this search we discover without pleasure how little courage we have.

The mind's quest for security presents conflicting images of the future, which can either inspire hope or provoke fear, as noted by C.S. Lewis (7). The great problem of the human being is that although he senses the power within us, we are hesitant to use it. But courage, like the other "flowers" in the garden of love, is in our inner universe and guides us in confronting the unknown and death, and achieving something unimaginable for others.

Many of us have experienced situations where we offered help to someone in need. This illustrates that we do possess courage.

Yet, if we reflect on the many times we imposed limitations or barriers on ourselves, or restrained expressing our opinions, we will see that we lack courage. Do we lose courage when we anticipate consequences? Whether these consequences exist or not, when we follow our intuition and save someone from peril, we simply act, without seeking reasons to refrain. Thus, courage is always present within us, as Mark Twain said: "Courage is not the absence of fear, but the mastery of it" (44).

To conquer fear, we must identify and understand its origins. By overcoming fear, we can find courage. We understand that courage has always existed within us but may have been suppressed by our inner baggage. We condition it when to go or not into action. When your courage wanes, you feel yourself losing love, and thus you activate the weapons of hatred and fear.

In such situations, we may lack the courage to express our feelings or desires to our loved ones but find the courage to throw all the "mess" that goes through our minds during arguments with him, to see that it hurts him. We harness the courage, we close his mouth.

Sometimes, we do this to avoid feeling small, weak, and worthless rather than to be pushed aside by those who want to love us or we do not feel their evil eyes and gossip directed at us.

Courage within us is the foundation of sincerity, truth, and respect. It is an inherent part of our being. Trust your instincts, take a stand, and do not allow selfish thoughts to hinder your soul. Let your courage speak for itself!

Responsibility

The thoughts and actions of all of us leave an impact on our reality, our nation, and the world as a whole. When words say one thing and deeds show something else, they express the chaos and confusion in which humanity is wanted to live. The facts speak beyond our thoughts about the responsibility we must shoulder.

In times of disappointment, it's common to question, "What can we do? This is just life." However, we actually, have a lot to do because, as Nicolae Iorga said, "Life is not just about living, but about understanding what you live for." (44)

In the numerous leaflets, and slogans used during political campaigns, great words and deeds are circulated, most of them being "dust in the eyes of the crowd". These "politicians" claim on paper to respect their peers, but their goal is their good. They publicly criticize each other, and behind the scenes, they collude for their own benefit. While they talk about the value of man and state it on paper, their actions are replaced by the thickness of the roll of banknotes (especially if they also have a good conversion on the financial market) and the shine of gold.

The next memory I want to share illustrates society's morality in terms of responsibility and is another example from my time working as a psychologist.

I remember flipping through the file in front of me, feeling disbelief each time as if I had never seen it before. It was hard to believe that such a file could enter the committee, let alone be approved. Not only was it missing one act, but it was missing most of them according to the law. Despite this, it was laid on the table and conveyed to me that it must be considered as it is. I even spoke to the person on the phone, asking him to bring the necessary documents, but he neither showed up with them nor sent any documents to the institution's address.

I put the file aside and put it on hold in the hopes that someone would decide to bring those documents, especially since "someone from above" suggested that we take care of him and put him on the list.

However, as time passed, weeks went by without any progress. The file did not follow the expected course, and it was not allowed to reach the committee.

One day, the door suddenly opens and she, the head of the committee enters thundering and lightning, speaking as the Romanian saying goes "like at the door of the tent". She asks why the file did not reach the committee and who had it on the list. I answered that it was me and she left suddenly. Then, shortly after, my direct boss enters the office, passing by my desk and says quietly, looking straight ahead:

"Be more careful, girls, whose doctor's signature and initials are on the papers in the file."

I understood that her words appealed to "my unfeeling heart" and I asked her:

"Why? Does the law somehow have two versions, one is for fools and one for the "great" ones, and I didn't take notice of it?"

It was not the first nor the last example of what I experienced there at the Directorate. Files accompanied by "rewards," completed with documents that came out like tape with the initials of doctors and psychologists, reached approval for "begging" a disability pension. People who said that they had something to eat, they had a situation, they came with "fake things" just to "pinch" some money. At first, I marvelled at those who had a higher position, therefore also a bigger pocket and still came to "beg". Then, slowly, slowly, I accepted that it was a painful reality of the world we live in.

This is how our selfishly driven society works and is governed by one and only god - money.

The question that many people face is what to do if their boss asks them to falsify documents, write untruths, or provide incorrect information. In my view, there are two options. First, you could refuse and face the consequences such as not being wanted at the institution anymore, being reprimanded, or being let go in a "civilised" manner. The other option is to comply with the request and pretend not to care, or appear as if you only want to please your bosses. However, there are people who are troubled by their conscience and face difficulties. Despite this, the action has already been taken and more irresponsibility has been added to our own lives and to the planet we live in, and it also leads to internal frustrations. In the end, we question the consequences of the diseases we have unleashed, not fully seeing the power lies within us, not others.

So, can we demand accountability from others if we don't provide it ourselves? And we wonder why is so much depression in our society?

It is common knowledge that serotonin is often referred to as the "hormone of happiness." As a central nervous system neurotransmitter, serotonin plays a role in transmitting signals between nerve cells and neurons. Symptoms of serotonin deficiency may include malaise, sleep disturbances, anxiety, and cravings for foods such as sweets or carbohydrates. Low levels of serotonin have been linked to decreased self-esteem and can contribute to feelings of violence. Recent studies suggest that depression may be associated with low levels of serotonin. Who do you think is responsible for the correct serotonin dosage? Bacteria in the intestines.

To wonder what happens in our mind and our world, if we are not responsible even for our body?

Genuine responsibility does not seek boundaries between us and the rest of the world, or to assign blame or find culprits, but rather stands as an inherent part of existence. One of the Laws of Zamolxis (41) offers a profound insight into this concept: "Be like the lofty mountain and raise your light above all that surrounds you. Remember that you take the same steps to its top as to its base; the air is the same above and below; the tree grows on the top of the mountain as well as at its base; the sun shines on the peak of the mountain as well as on the smooth earth."

Ultimately, the choice to embody this ideal is ours to make!

6. Soul Wealth

Beyond the passage of time and the contemplation of the gods, lies the Living and Eternal Fire, from which all things come and through which all things exisr. All and nothing are His breath, empty and full are His hands, motion and stillness are His feet, nowhere and everywhere His midst, and His face is light. Nothing is made without light, and everything that emerges from light comes to life and takes shape.

The Laws of Zamolxis *(41)*

Along with respect, truth and faith, responsibility is also part of the garden of love. Using each of them without looking for reasons to do so is understanding and using our inner wealth.

From the lessons of my life, I have learned that I can always look around me and have the power to make choices; I can be happy or I can be sad. I can choose to appreciate everything that life gives me because there are reasons I got them. I can enjoy the clearness of the sky, the warmth of the sunlight, the lush green of the leaves, the flight of the birds, the softness, the colors and the vibrant fragrance of the flowers. Alternatively, I can limit myself to seeing the negative aspects such as trash, meanness, hatred and greed. I can choose to live within the limits that society gives me because that's how I "have to", to be restless, angry, stressed and live in depression. I can look past all the negative aspects or happenings and see the good in every person, thing or event, because each of them helps to colour my life. As I have already said, life itself is not only good or bad, but a rainbow, a play of colours from the darkest to the lightest. We live through difficult times that can create inner storms, but that doesn't mean we can't find inner peace. It does not mean to fight with others, and not even with yourself, because in each of us, there is a warm light that, finding it, we can offer, and thus, leave a positive impact on the world.

Discovering that light, the warmth of the soul, you will hear its voice that is "simple", gentle, does not raise his tone, speak ironically, judge or blame, but only shows you the way. In the inner silence you will hear it more clearly.

In all that life offers us, we can choose to be a dull or dark colour and bathe in anger, malice, hatred, greed and revenge, or we can choose to be a warm one and colour the world as Pablo Picasso says, " Some painters turn the sun into a yellow spot, others turn a yellow spot into the sun." (44)

From childhood, we know that the sun is light and warmth. In the past, people saw much more than that in the sun. They looked at it with respect and worshiped it. It is now known to represent the heart of the solar system and signifies the masculine aspect of the creative force that exists within each of us. Its light and warmth lift our spirits. The yellow that represents it is a symbol of hope, joy, happiness, and trust. Also, wealth and royalty are associated with golden yellow. Johann Wolfgang von Goethe calls yellow "the color closest to light. In its highest purity, it always implies the nature of brilliance and has a joyful, serene, delicate, stimulating character. Therefore, experience teaches us that yellow gives a warm and comforting impression. (44)

W. W. Atkinson claims that yellow is the colour associated with our emotions. Depending on its brightness, it is linked to intellectual Power. For example, dark yellow represents an ordinary intellectual state, while true yellow signifies a sharp intellect. Atkinson also suggests that those showing "a high degree of True Occult Development exhibit a certain shade of yellow (38).

Regardless of one's choice, the colours we choose have an impact on those around us and on the entire world. If we seek a scientific explanation for this, we can turn to Fritoj Kapra (12), who explains that the properties of subatomic particles cannot be comprehended without understanding their interactions, and we will not be able to know one particle without knowing the others due to the intercorrelation of the atomic world.

Acting from the position of "I" and the rest of the world, we avoid the yellowness and warmth of the soul. For years, I neglected to love myself because I didn't know how. I thought I could conform to society's standards and be fine. Simply following others' advice that comes from their experience, wearing designer clothes or adorning yourself with makeup and jewellery doesn't equate to self-love.

To truly gauge how much you care for yourself, look into a mirror and focus on your eyes, not just your reflection. I didn't realize how challenging this could be. It's easy to look into someone else's eyes, but try doing it with yourself. Look into your eyes! I didn't think it was such a difficult task to do. To look at yourself and explore your inner self. Then, you'll confront your fear of what your eyes reveal, and the tendency to avoid facing your true self. Seek to uncover and embrace everything you hide within, and love every part of yourself.

It was difficult for me when I first started looking inside myself. However, by addressing my traumas and inner pain, I came to understand that I can find happiness in the little things in life, and I can try to see the positive side of everything. I've also learned to appreciate the beauty in each person, as I believe that no one is inherently evil. Instead, our experiences, environment, and internal struggles shape us. Besides, it's important to see that if we want to change the world, we must start with ourselves.

Amidst our inner struggles, a simple smile, a greeting, thank you, or an expression of gratitude can touch someone's soul. We have the power to spread positivity, much like offering a spot of yellow to the world, which can brighten and warm others like the sun. As Paganini once said, "The good, the truth, the beautiful, the soul composition of a man that finds echoes in the feelings of others, the whole range of relationships between people constitutes a rhythmic, closed chain." (4)

Love lessons

We often limit ourselves through negative thoughts and emotions. While negative thoughts can keep us chained in our own self-created hell, positive thoughts can break these chains and set us free. It's important to see our abilities, accept and love ourselves, and allow ourselves to grow. By understanding ourselves and setting our own limits, we can consciously set our limits and navigate our lives.

Our thoughts and emotions bring us lessons of love that we all receive and sometimes from where we least expect. They can come from unexpected sources in various ways. Some are repeated, because it depends on us whether we take them into account or not, but regardless of the lived experiences, I believe the most crucial lesson about love is understanding the closeness of death.

In theory, we all know that our days and hours are... numbered, because as Carlos Castaneda says, life is an arena in which there are only two fighters: man and death (6). However, our greatest mistake is our complacency in the feeling of immortality, due to being preoccupied with daily concerns. It's only when death approaches, the only irreversible aspect of our world, that we can see through the fog of our worries.

Even though "Death is not real even in the relative sense of the word; it is but the cradle of a new life." as it says in Kybalion (39), our greatest fear remains the fear of death. Often, we choose not to dwell on thoughts of mortality, as if by ignoring it, we can somehow evade its grasp.

We are all aware of the inevitability of death and the importance of living our lives with honesty and integrity. While this concept is widely acknowledged, it is those who have faced imminent death and been granted the opportunity to reflect on their lives during a reprieve who truly grasp the significance of their existence. Confronted with the acceptance that their time is finite, they contemplate what they might have done differently or not done at all. They might also consider how they wish to live if given more time.

It is easy to dispense advice, but personal experiences are incomparable. As life prepares to yield to death, we begin to see beyond the trivial concerns that have preoccupied us. It is the day we consciously acknowledge our mortality that we truly discern the most important aspects of our lives and the day we begin to truly live.

More than 25 years ago, I encountered an experience that forced me to face the idea of death head-on.

It was an autumn morning, and I was following my usual routine. I was living with my child in a room at a former high school dormitory. I was getting ready to go to school where I was a teacher, and had to wake up my child to go to classes as well. At one point, while taking a sip of coffee, I felt my head falling to one side. It happened a few times, which panicked me. I put the coffee down, sat down to calm myself, and tried again, but the head movement seemed much more violent. I had the feeling that my "mind" was falling. I can laugh now, but at that moment, I assure you I didn't feel like laughing. I was worried about what could happen and what direction my child's life would take if something happened to me. I woke up the child and told him as calmly as I could, given the situation, to get dressed and that he would go to school alone. I saw the immense fear in his eyes and knew what he was going to ask, so I explained that I wouldn't go to school with him because I might end up in the hospital. The child's eyes widened, and I could sense his deep fear. I went to the hospital, and my child stayed in the care of my next-door neighbour, who was a gipsy woman but always helped me whenever I neede. I am grateful to her as long as I live for everything she has done for me and my child.

At the hospital, I immediately had an EEG (electroencephalogram) due to my symptoms. I could hear everything that was being said, even though the people around me were trying to speak softly. The EEG showed very little activity in one part of my brain, so it was repeated with the same result. At the urging of the hospital staff, my sister, who was actually working as a nurse at the hospital, mobilised all her connections to arrange for a tomography. Because the situation was considered quite serious, there was a suspicion of a possible tumour. I was left wondering whether I would need surgery and suffer the consequences or just wait to die.

Shall I describe how much I cried? Shall I talk about how much I slept? At first, it seemed unfair to die so young, but my only concern was for my child. I loved him (and still do) with all my heart, I took care of him as best as I could, but I knew that I, his mother, was very important to him, no matter how much his grandmother loved him. His grandfather was no longer there, and from his father's side, aside from the name, there was no interest in the child.

Before going to the clinic for the CT scan, I quickly organized everything I knew and everything I could. After I left the hospital, the sensation of my head falling off was almost completely gone, but there was physical evidence from the electroencephalogram that something was wrong.

I cried enough for a lifetime, until I got to a clinic in a university centre. What did I think when I felt that death was around the corner? I thought about how hard I struggled for so many years, working seven days a week, at school and at home, to save money to buy a home, and to do everything right according to society's norms. I thought about how many of my own desires or my child's desires were postponed just to provide him with what I thought he needed: food and clothes. I prayed with rivers of tears just to be okay so I could raise my child and be happy with him. I hoped in case of a surgery, I would not be paralysed so as not to torment my child even more. To end this episode of my life, the CT scan showed absolutely nothing. I didn't, and we didn't feel like believing it.

Physically, I didn't die then, but my ego collapsed. I consciously realized how important the child was in my life, I as a mother for him and he for me. It wasn't the idea that I hadn't loved him until then, but the fact that I didn't know how to show him the love he needed, being in a constant rush for what is needed to live "well". I understood that not only had I not lived well, but I had also not followed the path I wanted.

Thus, the words of Irvin D. Yalom (14) were confirmed to me; facing death can bring us many benefits. Beyond the idea that "death is as natural as life" as Arthur Schopenhauer says, it is no longer just something abstract for us, but a close presence that we cannot ignore, as Oliver Sacks describes (30). The idea of death forces us to honestly evaluate the journey we had taken up to that moment. Did we do what we wanted? Do we feel fulfilled? Do we have regrets? What can we change and do differently going forward? What else can we do to make peace with ourselves?

It was years later when the child confided in me about how much he cried during those days. He concealed his tears and prayed for his mother's health. He told me that while crying, he was making promises that he didn't want any more toys or anything else because he knew I was saving money for buying a house. He made promises, exchanging them for my life beside him. These experiences reminded me of the words of Thomas à Kempis, who said, "Love is ever awake, never weary of work, nor oppressed by suffering, nor discouraged by fear." (44)

I discovered the hard way that we truly appreciate life only when we are on the brink of losing it. I runderstood that even if I had a mountain of gold, I wouldn't trade it for love. The unconditional love of my child and our wish to be there for each other throughout our lives. I experienced firsthand the theory that at any given moment, life could end. I came to understand that while the thought of death frightened me, the idea of death saved me.

The most important lesson is to know that you will die, but it is much more important to live, knowing that you will die without regrets and what we leave behind is not houses and cars, not money and fortunes, but... love. The stronger the feeling that the life we live is not good, the greater the terror of death, says Irvin D. Yalom (14). We only have one chance to live this life, and it is best to live it fully in order to leave with as few regrets as possible.

I'm not the only one who lived for years as if I were following some scripts, following some patterns. But because life is so much more than that, I learned lessons of love from my mistakes and selfishness. Somewhere within I knew, and I still know today, that what I experienced at that time was for me to return to what defines us all: love. Rainbows come and go, but our love does not disappear because it just exists within us, being part of infinite love.

Love

Each of us has our own way of seeing the world and understanding the mystery of life. In this quest, people have used not only the mystical and scientific approaches, as Fritoj Kapra (12) mentions, but also poetry, mythology, and the path of the shaman, each offering different models of an aspect of the world. However, none of these approaches provides a complete picture of the world.

In the same way, we can say that we do not have a complete answer to the question, "What is love?" I don't know if you can say there is a better or lesser answer. People have used the softness of colours, the harmony of lyrics and musical notes, and have written and expressed their own vision of what love can be. Each being gives its own answer because it experiences and understands it in its own unique way. Some have lived and died for love, but we cannot say that we have an exact definition of love.

I was talking in another chapter about Nicolae Iorga's exhortation to live your life, knowing what you live it for. If in the past I thought that having money and possessions made me happy, one day I understood how much I was lying to myself. I got to the point where I pretty much lost everything I had. I have come to understand that life is more than a job, money, and retirement.

Following intuition directs us on a certain path, on which we have a mission to fulfil in this world, which is related to the mission of each of us. In this way, we come to understand that respecting each other, being honest with each other, and telling each other the truth is what we call "love". It's hard for us to believe, because in our eyes, love is only linked to the couple, children, family, but if we think about all the teachings that come from ancient times, they all urge us to return to ourselves, to the source of love. The Emerald Tablets of Thoth the Atlantean (40) say, "If you live among men, make Love all to your heart."

Even those who dedicate their lives to the inner good of man admit, at some point, that without love and compassion, you cannot reach the soul of man and help him with his pains. Among them the psychiatrist Irvin D. Yalom (14) stated that until a certain moment, he had not dared to use the words "love" and "compassion" in discussions about the practice of psychotherapy. But in his journey to himself, he understood that by paying attention to the presence or absence of these feelings for patients, he had many more opportunities to help them. As another example, he considers trying to answer all of his fan mail as a daily form of Buddhist meditation focused on love and compassion.

No matter how we express ourselves, where love is given power, it rules. We can all say that we feel love coming from within us.

Whether we say "my soul hurts", "you filled my soul with joy" or "I feel like my soul is exploding with joy", we have a simple answer about what we feel, our emotions, and how we perceive our connection to the surrounding world.

By saying you love life, that includes everything around us. It does not only include the things that, in your selfishness, you think you own and belong to you. Moreover, to love is not to possess. It means respecting everything and giving that respect. If we take the box or jar, for example, in which we collected money as children, we collected to spend on something we wanted. As adults, we have messed up the balance and we are focused only on accumulating, and we forget or don't want to give anymore. However, we all come into this life to learn to truly love. No matter how many things we struggle with, no matter how many people we try to have around us to feel loved, true love will emerge when we begin to love ourselves and thus, we will be able to see the selfishness that seeks to accumulate as much as possible and give as little or nothing. In return, truly loving means giving unconditionally, without thinking if, when, and how you will get something back.

*We all go through experiences as much as we need to learn our lessons to become what we are at the core – love. Many prefer to remain prisoners of fear and ignorance, they prefer darkness. Others choose the light of knowledge and love because they know that only these break the chains, says Patricia Cori (33). For this, we need to look fearlessly into the darkness we live and which we came to experience precisely to see the light within us and learn **what love is. In a sense, we live our lives seeking the light of knowledge.** When we* *are ready to start digging through the darkness within ourselves, we find the light, because light comes from* **love***.*

On the scale of emotions, love has the highest vibration. Perhaps this is where the expression "we walk with our heads in the clouds" comes from. We live this life to learn to love, and we all know that when we love, we feel alive. Moreover, we cannot give advice to the heart or draw laws and directives on what and whom to love. Love just is.

Love just exists and is boundless. It needs no strategies, and no strategy succeeds before it. It needs no rulers because it rules by its very existence. Furthermore, where love is present, there is no desire for power.

Many say they love because that is what their faith teaches them. But is it love when they despise those who do not share their belief or try to impose it on them through various methods? When you disrespect another person's beliefs, no matter what they are, their opinion, trying to prove them wrong.

To love means to respect and accept each person with their opinions, beliefs, desires, and dreams, even if they don't make any sense or seem silly to you. Inside every human is a place of wordless knowledge that each of us can access.

To love is to give your love without expectations. When love becomes selfish by conditioning it with other thoughts, feelings or deeds, it loses its true essence. Using terms of comparison for love makes it conditional again, but true love has no terms of comparison; it is all-encompassing.

We can re-learn true love from children. They are pure and sincere when they say "I love you". They say it wholeheartedly, without restriction, without fear that they might be rejected, or that the person in front of them doesn't love them. You can see their love in the sparkle of their eyes, those mirrors of the soul. They love unconditionally. Instead, as adults, we often live according to patterns, conforming to the expectations of others, despite Cicero's advice is "Do not leave your nature to conform to another's life." (44).

When we depart from our uniqueness, we give our focus and energy to those we fear disappointing or upsetting, rather than focusing on ourselves. We focus our attention on blaming others for the challenges we face. Being preoccupied with what others are doing and not with us, it takes us off the course of our lives and we miss the "now" moment, the point where time meets eternity as C. S. Lewis says (7), but time is the same for all of us or how says Kahlil Gibran, "It is known that today is but the memory of yesterday, while tomorrow is the dream of the present moment." (17)

We have the power to decide how we spend our time, especially considering that we don't know how much time we have on this earth. So why spend our present living in others' shadows and their actions?

In romantic love, if your partner doesn't respond to your feelings as you hoped, you might feel angry, and frustrated, and believe that they don't love you the same way. You might start searching for reasons or ways to make them feel the way you do. You start looking for causes, reasons or ways of revenge to control their thoughts and feelings. You think he doesn't deserve to be loved the way you love him because he doesn't reciprocate your feelings. This behaviour comes from selfishness, not love. Each person has different experiences, desires, and views on love in a relationship. Trying to control your partner's feelings, desires, dreams, and actions shows a lack of respect for their personal space. According to the knowledge within us, as part of the universal consciousness, everyone has other experiences, other desires, and other views on everything, including love in a couple. Trying to control the feelings of the person next to you, their feelings, desires, dreams, and actions, you don't even respect their personal space, and control is born from fear, not love. It is a fear of not being good enough, us or the partner. To it, we add the fear of not being loved as you think you love, the fear of not being abandoned, the fear of living alone... Only fears but true love is suffocated by them, by needs, expectations, frustrations, and weeds of selfishness. True love does not live where fears breathe, grow and increase. It means the confident communication of fears and feelings with our partner means, according to Allan Pease (3), increasing the level of security that the woman feels and a minimum level of infidelity on the part of the man.

Nor is it true love where you disrespect your child's desire for privacy, his thoughts, to follow the path he wants. You love him only with your mind. You tell him what to do without considering what he wants to do. Don't let him experience anything that would make him experience other life lessons than what you, his parent, think he needs. You make your child the bearer of your dreams and aspirations. We say it's love, but it's selfish. Each of us is unique and so are our experiences. We are on earth to live our own lives. Other people's experiences are not ours, just as ours are not other people's. The emotions we live in each experience differ, they are unique like us, but our world today is the result of our thoughts, emotions and actions

By assuming and fulfilling the role you came to play on the great stage of humanity, each one contributes to changing the world because each of us has our own impact on it. Throughout history, many who have opposed manipulation and betrayal in one way or another have been sentenced to death. Whether justified or not, the convictions have remained inscribed in the humanity's collective memory as shocks and, according to Schopenhauer (5), as simple acts of destruction of life that annihilate the will to live.

Authorities and justice instil fear of death through laws and punishments. The Church also contributes to this fear by framing your sufferings, worries, and needs as punishments for simply existing. You're led to believe that as a "sinner," you will be punished and sent to hell, or that if you don't love, you will face punishment. Love driven by fear is conditional, while true love is condemned as a sin. The notion of eternal hell as a punishment, taught to children by some teachers and priests, is just one form of emotional abuse (35) resulting from conditional love. Making love in a couple is a sin (in certain days, periods), although you cannot dictate to the senses when to do it and in addition, this is the way to create the miracle called "child".

True love is boundless and unconditional. It transcends all constraints and doesn't require any strategies to thrive. It transcends religious boundaries as it is the very essence of humanity's religion. It doesn't need any authority to govern because it rules through its mere existence. Furthermore, where love reigns, the thirst for power is nonexistent.

True love knows no bounds and no barriers. The most enduring example of this is a mother's love for her child. Nature also provides us with examples, such as the love between the pairs of swans, doves, as well as the devotion of a dog to its owner.

Love is an invincible and powerful force. Man is a centre of living mental energy in the Great Ocean of Energy, says W. W. Atkinson (38), and his soul is pure love, says David Icke (9), and where the light of love shines, thieves do not enter, because "they have afraid of being seen, says Omraam Mikhael Aivanhov: "They wait for everything to be extinguished and for the residents to sleep before enter the house. Things happen the same in a country and within the man himself. If you extinguish the lamps (that is, the virtues) in yourselves, thieves come and bind you faithfully, that is, your freedom and everything you consider precious are taken from you. Thieves are diseases, suffering, negative thoughts, troubles, etc... Only the light can protect us because it is the true guardian: no one can approach without being seen..." (31).

Where the light of love is extinguished, faces are gloomy, and you will find stiffness, misery, and the earth stripped of its garments as a picture of anger, hatred, and carelessness. The negativity equates to the darkness we live in and project into the world through our thinking and actions. Many among us (I have been one of them) talk continually of troubles, cares, and diseases, people whose presence W. W. Atkinson calls depressing (38). We seek to avoid them because we feel their "darkness" and neither their presence nor their thoughts do us any good.

We live amidst troubles, worries, pains, and illnesses, and yet we place a monetary value on everything and are willing to exchange anything for a price. But can genuine love be bought with money? Wealth is fleeting. You can trade your mind and body for money and tell lies for it, but deep down, if you listen to the voice of your soul, you'll feel that you cannot love on command, because "love cannot be forced." If you found yourself in a situation where you had to save a loved one, you "give everything" you have externally just to know that he is healthy and by your side.

But also in relationships, we can fall into extremes. Some of us do everything we can to salvage a relationship without understanding that once it doesn't work, even after we've made some attempts to get it back on track or find a different path, it's time to let it go. Nothing lasts forever... Have you considered that maybe your partner no longer wants the relationship, or that you are investing too much in it while the balance in the relationship has vanished? Perhaps you are the one who wants to leave the relationship and are struggling to express your feelings, or are afraid of loss or loneliness and don't want to acknowledge your desire to leave.

Emotions are felt differently by the two. The balance of the relationship has been disrupted, or perhaps it never existed. Maybe what brought us together was just the identical vibrational frequency of the emotions we had inside of us and we had no idea, but we lied ourselves that we loved each other. As much as we would like to, we are not the same and we cannot coexist as long as no emotion connects us, as long as we no longer vibrate on the same frequency. Thus, the reasons that lead one of the partners to the desire to break free from the existing relationship do not have to be shared with the partner, especially since our needs as women and men are different.

As long as there is no harmony in the relationship when the balance of the couple has broken or does not exist, the children suffer. When parents verbally and/or physically harm each other, they bring no benefit to the children, and their behaviour becomes the root of these children's traumas. Moreover, the latter suffer the most from such a rupture, because they do not understand what is happening, or if they do, the understanding is made only through the lens of their fragile knowledge.

The emotions that connect us as parents to our children can vary from person to person. We are emotion, but we vibrate differently depending on our emotional stores. Schopenhauer gives us the example of the bird that feels good in the air, of the fish in the water, of the mouse in the ground and thus, we humans too, experience each event in our life differently because we each have our own "atmosphere".

We often use expressions like "I don't know where that came from" or "they don't take after either parent." , but we also know the saying "where you give and where it breaks". It is not always valid, but as with everything, "the exception confirms the rule". If you've ever split logs, you've seen that you hit one side with the ax and the wood cracks in another. The pieces of wood bounce to one side or the other, they don't all fall to the same side or the same distance. The same with us humans, and the above expressions denote deeply rooted beliefs in man. Does the child have to look like his parents? If he doesn't we can't love him? We come from generation to generation and have the ancestral heritage, to which are added our own experiences and perceptions. However, we still want to make these children like us. To look like us, to act like us, to go to whatever school we want. But if they are not "us", why do we have to impose our personal rules on them? Whether you haven't fulfilled a dream, don't try to make someone else live it for you. Your child did not come into this life to worship you with his life.

Going back to breaking logs, each piece of wood that come out of that log will vary in size. The life of each of us has a certain duration on this earth. Don't we come and leave this life together, and then shouldn't it be lived as each wants?

Decisions motivated by selfishness are not genuine acts of love. Being selfish leads to thoughts like "he doesn't deserve my love". But who determines worth? Is it your expectations or those of others? Do you have the right to judge someone's worth? How do you measure the love you give and receive? Is your love selfless or selfish? True love has no conditions, no arguments, and no judgment.

Every being desires to be loved. Many people just ask for it and take it, but from a bag that you keep taking to give something to someone, at some point you will feel that you have nothing left to offer, and not because you lack love. You feel like you've tried everything you knew or could do. In order to change something, you need to set boundaries. I repeat, this doesn't mean you lack love, as love is infinite, but it's about trusting and respecting yourself. That way, you will stop and understand that the other person may only want to receive, without understanding the need to give in order to receive, or they may be too selfish to do so.

Love cannot be measured or weighed. It has no units of measure and does not need a scale. It needs nothing and costs nothing, because it just exists.

To a soul that gives sincere love, simplicity will be more valuable than the brilliance of diamonds. A mother does not seek to be paid for the love she gives her child all her life. She loves her "baby" regardless of what they face and regardless of their age. A puppy loves its master unconditionally. Only we humans complicate things and give dimensions created by our minds to the immensity that surrounds us, as Carlos Castaneda (6) says.

On the other hand, love knows no obstacles and no conditions. You love the person next to you, you smile at the person you meet, you respect your own truth, you set your own limits, and you accept that change is inevitable in everyone's life because life has ups and downs. It is a process that involves birth, evolution, and death. Nothing is permanent, for change, according to the teachings of the Kybalion (39), means creation and destruction, building and tearing down, action and reaction. What is around us is a continuous change, an appearance, "the outward manifestation of a hidden power, of a Substantial Reality," as also called in the Kybalion (39).

Instead of focusing on the negative, try to find the good in every situation in your life. Instead of causing harm, choose to do good. Instead of consuming negative news, listen to music, take a walk in nature, or plant a flower or a tree. Engage in activities that bring you joy, as these are the things that lead to the happiness coveted by everyone, because the pleasure, the passion, the good, all reside in you, or as W. W. Atkinson says, instead of becoming a "beggar of nature" you can become a Master of it (38).

True love cannot be bought or sold. It helps you understand that every individual is a reflection of you in different dimensions and lives with their own dreams and desires. Love is not something you own, nor is it a copy of you. If you do not love yourself, you will seek love in vain from others. What you don't do for yourself, no one else will do for you.

The sun, the moon, the flowers, the trees, the wind, and the ocean do not impose conditions on us to appreciate their beauty and love. They simply share what they know, which is love from the cosmic source. When we unconditionally enjoy the wonders that our souls offer, we align with the universe, feel true love, and can also give love unconditionally.

Regardless of the version we experience, we leave our energetic imprint on society, and the world carries everyone's energetic imprint through our thoughts and emotions. We are interconnected with the world, and the world is united with us. By changing ourselves, we can change the world.

Gratitude

I was discussing the principle of polarity formulated in the Kybalion (39). We can find the polarity of love in hate. Vibrationally we find its opposite in fear, but if we believe there is no term of comparison, we cannot evaluate it, or measure it, because love just exists, shouldn't the opposite of love be gratitude? Love involves giving respect and taking responsibility, it embodies compassion, and through gratitude, we reciprocate and give it all back, thus, we both receive and give love. It is reciprocity as Joan Wilcox calls it, and it is the sacred principle of reciprocity that the Incas speak of. Even in the self-centredness of our society, we strive to give something back to the person who has done us a favour, to repay their kindness. We give because we receive, and in giving, we receive.

Love and gratitude together are considered the greatest healers. It's important to note that we're referring to gratitude that comes from the heart, from sincerity and our truth. It isn't conditioned by petty interests and doesn't have any requirements regarding the creation you are grateful for. You can be grateful for a flower that appeared in your field of vision and dispelled the sadness you felt before seeing it. You can be thankful for the tree that provides shade on a hot day. You can express gratitude for the food you eat, the water you drink, and the living beings around you.

I once worked with a young deputy manager at a home for children with epilepsy and autism in the UK. Despite being younger than me, he was very dedicated to his work and had a playful and caring nature. He had a love for jokes, music, and all living things. Whenever he found a spider in the house, he would gently pick it up and release it outside, showing gratitude for its existence.

Many of us find it challenging to be grateful to other forms of life, especially to creatures like spiders. We often reserve gratitude for family members or strangers who do us favours. It's difficult to see someone who has wronged you as an equal and to offer them kindness. It is not easy to see an equal in another creature. It is not easy to get over the weed of ego. To give good to the one who harms you, grinds your pride and displeases selfishness. It loses ground. You think that you will be seen as a weak or "stupid" person if you turn the other cheek to the person who did something bad to you. On the other hand, you don't feel good when you are in the position of the other and you want to be treated nicely and to be offered good, gratitude, thanks. By learning to put ourselves in the position of another, we see that we do not like to have done to us what we do to another. And yet, how do we behave with the rest of the people around us? How do we treat animals? The forests? The waters of the planet? By recognizing the value of every living being and being grateful for their existence, we can learn to treat others with kindness, including animals and the environment. It requires setting aside our egos and selfishness. Showing kindness to those who have harmed us might hurt our pride, but it's important to put ourselves in their shoes and consider how we would want to be treated. Embracing the truth that every creature has its own worth allows us to cultivate gratitude for who they are.

The phrase "thank you" is a genuine way to express gratitude. Similarly, saying "I'm sorry" and "forgive me" are expressions that carry positive energy, benefiting both the speaker and the recipient. It costs nothing to use these expressions, except for perhaps a little self-consciousness. If you find it challenging to use these words, consider the reasons behind your reluctance. What is holding you back from using these expressions? Where does this resistance come from?

Gratitude is a way to reciprocate the love we receive. Each time you say "thank you", you are expressing gratitude and sending positive energy out into the universe. Surprisingly, these expressions are underused in our world, or used insincerely, often out of obligation, because "we have to", "it is nice to say it", rather than genuine feelings. In reality, those word can accompany any action in our lives, and when we truly understand and practice genuine forgiveness, expressing gratitude becomes second nature. This allows us to be thankful not only for the good things we receive in life, but also for everything life offers us. Oliver Sacks believed he was blessed with wonderful things and in return, he shared his inner wealth with the world, as gratitude remained a predominant feeling within him.

By treating with gratitude even those you feel have wronged you, you accept that they were just the universe's tool in giving you the lessons you need to learn from in this life. Thanking to whatever was or is bad in your life, neither pride nor malice prevails. I can't even say that you will win because love doesn't live for that. It just exists, but you will feel free and at peace with yourself.

Give thanks to the earth, sky, wind, rain and sun, flowers and trees for all the joy, beauty and blessings they bring to your life. Everything is energy and everything has the same right as me, as you, to be here on earth. By giving love, we receive love back. This is the principle of Ayni, a law of love.

7. Love Garden

Fire, the inner fire, is the most powerful of all force, for it overcomes all things and penetrates to all things on the Earth.
The Emerald Tablets of Thoth the Atlantean (40)

Our Inner Wealth

Whether discussing forgiveness and love, or respect and gratitude, each of these flowers represents a part of our inner garden. We all seek to receive them and often look for them outside of ourselves, but they actually exist within all of us at all times, just waiting to be nurtured and shared with the world.

Whether we receive them from those close to us or from people we only meet briefly along our life's journey, the fragrance, colour, and tenderness of any flower we receive makes us feel respected, loved, rich, and worthy. What if we could give these flowers without expecting to receive them in return? What if we didn't worry about if, when, and from whom we would receive them? What if, when we desire them but don't receive them, we don't become upset, or look for reasons to argue with others, or judge our peers by the "face and likeness" of our thoughts?

It is not easy to forgive, respect, love, or help someone who you believe has wronged you. To uproot the weeds of selfishness, you need to see how harmful it is and how much harm it does to those around you, loved ones or strangers. You will need to see how much harm you have done to yourself in the first place because you have suffered or are suffering for things you do not know how to explain because you lack the knowledge of the mind or do not trust the wisdom of the soul.

Often, we are unaware of the harm we cause to those around us. But we don't do it because we intend to hurt people or other beings. We do it because it's the only way we know how to live. It's how we're taught from the time we start to understand what's going on around us. It's just that there comes a time in everyone's life when you feel you need to decide whether to continue the "charade" you're playing with your own life, or to take control and change direction.

When you live from a false trust in yourself and others, driven by a false love that is conditioned by false lack and pain, you may think you love someone. In this way, you give up a lot of things for that person and at some point, you feel empty inside. You come to the understanding that you are not living your own life, but living the life of an "I", built from directions provided by others, from procrastination, from lack of respect and self-love. You understand that all those compromises made in that relationship do not define the person you thought you were or wanted to be, but the person someone else wants you to be. Besides, living solely to fulfil someone else's desires, even a partner's, can leave you feeling depleted and disconnected from yourself.

We often make compromises born from our inner baggages. I have mentioned on other occasions, that at some point, my frustrations led me to leave the country in search of the "happiness" everyone desires. After years, I realized that working for money and wealth wasn't what I truly wanted because they weren't my motivation for living where I was and doing what I was doing. Then my decision to return home led to the breakup of my family. Although I was aware that new beginnings require sacrificing something "old", only at that moment I understood that the "old" thing was my marriage. My pain was huge because I was afraid of what I was experiencing although it was not the first time I was in that position. But the pain came from what I was taught as a woman, that I am not "valuable" as long as I don't have "the other half" with me. That a woman is only worthy when she has a man by her side.

Returning home on my own helped me understand that I am not a "half" and never was. It brought me to the position of understanding that no one is only "half". Thinking this way, everything we do seems to be done only in half measures, conditioned by everything we have negative in us, by the pains of the inner baggage that we were not taught to get rid of. I learned that I am a whole, a person born worthy, and a woman who can stand on her own feet without another "half" by my side. I learned that I am a complete and valuable individual who has the right to live life on my own terms.

I understood that I had been living according to societal expectations without truly listening to myself. My marriage had been a compromise to avoid being alone, a compromise made with a man who lived like me, between the limits imposed by selfish societal patterns.

In such a marriage, even if we said we loved each other, that love was false because it was born from the boundaries we are taught to live within to comply with society's norms. Unconsciously, we imposed limits on each other, because we were two "halves" in search of love, without knowing that we could not give what we did not have for ourselves. After all, a "half" cannot offer what a "whole" can. I did not know what and how true love feels, built on its basic principles, respect, forgiveness, and truth, without limitations imposed by the fears in which I had lived. Besides, when you love yourself, you can't accept someone else's limits on you. You set your own barriers and are aware that you are a "whole" without accepting someone else's control and manipulation.

Upon the news that I am returning to the country, most of the people I know, including "friends", and colleagues, told me that my return is "stupid". I was living a life that I had and in which I had "everything a man wants", meaning here a job, a house, cars, money. I lost my so-called marriage and returned to the country, where I had nothing but a roof over my head. I had nothing of what I once had, but that nothing meant more than what I had abroad. Indeed, it all seemed crazy, but I had never felt freedom as it was at that moment. I didn't know what I would do, where I would go, or how I would live, but everything crystallised, step by step. I only had a few people around me who believed in me, but they represented more than anything I had ever had before.

Going down this path was not easy. At the start, I felt like I would never get over the pain of separation, and I shed countless tears. As I reflected on the reasons, emotions, and acceptance, emerging from the dark abyss I had been thrown into, I was able to see the beauty in the time I spent with my ex-husband. I understood that we had both been instruments and played important roles in each other's lives. I understood once again that nothing, not even a marriage, is guaranteed "till death do us apart." This experience taught me that everything can start anew, that a person who was once your partner can become a good friend or simply a passerby in your life.

Building my self-confidence, which I never had as a result of a lack of support from childhood and throughout my life, required a lot of work. I struggled with my inner demons stemming from feelings of inadequacy as a being and as a woman. After years of seeking validation through education and degrees, I came to understand that my worth as a human isn't defined by papers, money, or the opinions of others. The diplomas and certificates I earned did not define my true value because that is not external; it resides within you, me and each of us.

*Love conditioned by money, social status, or external validation is not true love. It is **a love on a stage of selfishness, where each one suffers in his own way and hurts himself and harms others***

to prove the value he looks for outside of himself. *When you consider yourself not good enough, that you don't have enough, you may seek love from others to fill this void, when you don't even love yourself.*

However, when you genuinely love and accept yourself, you can also love your partner wholeheartedly, embracing their dreams, desires, and decisions that make them happy. In a healthy relationship, each person is a complete individual and life together can be a whole squared.

True love is not about control, but the freedom to be who you are. It does not require ego control, impose conditions that limit self-gratification, or confine us within the bounds of marriage or how we choose to live our lives. Like the dance of a tango, it takes two, each moving in their own way but following the same rhythm. I feel loved when my partner sees and respects me as a "whole", a complete person, rather than trying to change me into the person they want me to be, or vice versa.

Some argue that this is not true, as our world is filled with hate and anger. However, it is true because it is what we emanate and live by accepting a selfish love, or shifting to an unconditional one. As Patricia Cori (33) mentions, everything we create exists in our electromagnetic field and reflects back to us, becoming part of our energy signature as our angels and demons. If we cultivate anger and fear, we will receive them back and live in our own hell. Conversely, by following our hearts, we can live in our own heaven. We are the creators of our own hell or heaven; they are simply a manifestation of our choices. We have the power to shape our reality and change the world. We are not condemned by anyone or anything; we condemn ourselves.

True love is an act of mutual respect and trust between two "whole" people. It involves two individuals with their own dreams and inner strength who support each other without fear or a desire for control.

To live differently than we have in the past, we need to see the darkness in which we have lived and the lies have surrounded us. This has been ingrained in us since childhood, but unlike previous generations, we have the opportunity to educate ourselves through books and the internet. We can seek out knowledge that resonates with us to find our inner wealth.

Love just is. It exists naturally, was not created with and for money. It is part of ONE's love, and it is unconditional. It can be found in places where human creations harmonize with nature, where children laugh joyfully, and the elderly are respected. It is also found in the act of sharing a piece of bread with a puppy. Be sure that the key to love is not found in money, regardless of one's wealth. It resides within your soul, as Thoth the Atlantean says, "the key to the worlds within you is found only within you." (40)

Can you imagine a garden without flowers? A flower stalk without leaves, without an inflorescence? A tree without leaves? This is what a person without emotions would look like. Emotions are the flowers that color and beautify our lives. The emotions we let bloom in us, although spontaneous because we don't choose them, are directed by our thoughts.

Just like if a seed we plant in our garden is good, if we don't give it everything it needs, it will dry up and die in the ground. So it is with our actions. If you grow flowers and care for them, you will enjoy their colour, fragrance, and beauty. If you leave the garden in ruins, you will welcome dryness and weeds, and the seed you want will not sprout where the weeds are the masters. If it sprouts, it will be suppressed by weeds, their shade, and height. Thus the flowers of your life are condemned to darkness, though they yearn for light while the poison dripped from fear is within you. Removing the negative weeds from our minds is not an easy job, but it will leave room for positive thoughts, which, watered and nurtured, will grow unhindered.

Will you feast your eyes on what others have in their garden? Will you dare to weed your garden and make room for flowers? We can plant the seeds or let the wind, rain, and earth take care of them. The choice is yours! W. W. Atkinson says that only when fear is eradicated, care, hatred, anger, malice, and all other weeds die, will your mental garden bloom in the luxuriance of beauty and joy (38). Re-entering the path of the self, finding our harmony, following and putting into practice the laws of life, we will not sit, as they say in Kybalion (39), at "a rich table in front of which we die of hunger".

We often allow ourselves to be driven by the power and relentless desire for power of the ego. However, we can live simply by following the love and light within us. We have the power to love, express love, and pass it on. By following the law of love or living against it, we will live and bear the consequences of our actions. In truth, we will reap what we sow in our own garden, and the beauty of your garden and your happiness does not depend on anyone outside of you. Accept that you are the gardener of your own life. Sow in your garden what YOU want to reap!

Everything I have shared with you in this book represents my truth. If it resonated with you, maybe you'll look for a way to find your own path. If it didn't resonate with you, you might seek to criticize me. You won't be the first and maybe not the last. However, no matter how much you may dislike what I've written, you will not change my experiences, feelings, perception, and beliefs. Even if you throw mud at me, I can't be you, just as you can't be me. My lines represent the loyalty of my soul, offering you love and appreciation for the being that you are, like flowers in a garden.

Do not expect to receive from others what you do not give. Don't wait to pick the empty branches of regret before death! Remember, the most beautiful flowers grow in the garden of love. Give them as long as you live, because they are free, or as Constantin Brâncuşi says, "Love calls love. It is not so important to be loved as to love with all your might and all your being." (44)

References

1. *Alice Miller - Deșteptarea Evei - Despre vindecarea orbirii emoționale, format PDF descărcat de pe internet;*

2. *Alice Miller - Revolta Trupului, Editura Nemita & Co, București, 2006;*

3. *Allan Pease - De ce Bărbații au nevoie de Sex, iar Femeile de Dragoste, format PDF descărcat de pe internet;*

4. *Anatolii Vinogradov - Defăimarea lui Paganini, Opera Română în colaborare cu Editura Muzicală, Craiova, 1987, pg. 351, 351;*

5. *Arthur Schopenhauer - Viața, amorul, moartea, format PDF descărcat de pe internet, pg. 6, 25, 80, 35, 25, 26, 36, 82;*

6. *Carlos Castaneda - Puterea Tăcerii, RAO International Publishing Company, Grupul Editorial RAO, București, 2000, format PDF descărcat de pe internet, pg. 160;*

7. *Clive Staples Lewis - Sfaturile unui diavol bătrân către unul mai tânăr, Editura Humanitas, București, 2007;*

8. *Dan D. Farcaș - De ce tac civilizațiile extraterestre, Editura Albatros, București, 1983;*

9. *David Icke - Secretul Suprem, vol 1 & 2, format PDF descărcat de pe internet;*

10. *Dominique Webb - Drumul spre success, Rom Direct Impex srl, 1994;*

11. *Doreen Virtue - How to hear your Angels, Hay House UK Ltd, Croydon, 2007;*

12. *Fritoj Kapra - Teofizica, Editura Tehnică, București, 2004, pg. 82;*

13. *Harald W. Tietze - Terapia cu apă - Modalitate străveche, eficientă și gratuită de vindecare, Editura Mix, 2017, pg. 56;*

14. *Irvin D. Yalom - Călătoria către sine - memoriile unui psihiatru, Editura Vellant, 2017, Versiune ebook: v1.0, august 2019;*

15. *Jamie King - 111 Teorii ale conspirației, format PDF descărcat de pe internet;*

16. *Jean-Jacques Servan- Schreiber - Sfidarea mondială, Editura Politică, București, 1982;*

17. *Kahlil Gibran - The Prophet, format PDF descărcat de pe internet, pg. 3, 12;*

18. *Lao Tze - TAO TE KING sau Cartea Cărării Supremului Adevăr, format PDF descărcat de pe internet, pg. 11, 4, 8;*

19. *Laurent Gounelle - Ziua în care am învățat să mă iubesc, Editura Trei, 2018 Versiune ebook: v1.0, ianuarie 2019, format PDF descărcat de pe internet;*

20. *Lise Bourbeau - Ascultă-ți corpul, prietenul tău cel mai bun, format PDF descărcat de pe internet;*

21. *Lyall Watson - Supernature - A natural history of the supernatural, 1992, format PDF descărcat de pe internet.*

22. *Masaru Emoto - Miracolul Apei, Editura Adevăr Divin, Brașov, 2007,*

23. *Mateo Sol - https://lonerwolf.com*

24. *Napoleon Săvescu - Noi nu suntem urmașii Romei, Editura Intact, București, 2002, pg. 122, 128, 150;*

25. *Neale Donald Walsch - Ce vrea Dumnezeu - Un răspuns fundamental la cea mai mare întrebare a omenirii, Editura For You, 2009;*

26. *Neville Goddard - Legea și făgăduința, G. & J. PUBLISHING CO. Los Angeles, California, 1961, pg. 5;*

27. *Neville Goddard - Rugăciunea, Arta de a crede, G & J PUBLISHING CO. Los Angeles, California, 1945, pg. 4, 16, 20, 10, 20, 4;*

28. *Norman Cousins - Anatomy of an Illness as Perceived by the Patient, Reflections on Healing and Regeneration, Bantam Books, Toronto, New York, London, 1979;*

29. *Okakura Kakuzo - The Book of Tea, New York: Putnam's, Originally Published in 1906, pg. 34, 31, 15, 15, 36, 29, 17, 12;*

30. *Oliver Sacks - Recunoștință, Editura Humanitas, 2017, versiune: e-book, v1.0, ianuarie 2019;*

31. *Omraam Mikhael Aivanhov - Iubire, înțelepciune și adevăr (Gura, urechile și ochii), Conferința din 05.03.1938 (Paris), format PDF descărcat de pe internet;*

32. *Patricia Cori - The New Sirian Revelations, Galactic Prophecies for the Ascending Human Collective, North Atlantic Books, Berkeley, California, 2017;*

33. *Patricia Cori - Universul Sufletului - Un apel de trezire către umanitate, Editura Salco, Brașov, 2010;*

34. *Pavel Coruț - Singuri sub Crucea Nordului, Editura Miracol, București, 1994, pg. 8;*

35. *Richard Dawkins - Dumnezeu o amăgire, format PDF descărcat de pe internet;*

36. *Terry Cole-Whittaker - What You Think Of Me Is None Of My Business, Jove Books, New York, 1979;*

37. *William Walker Atkinson - Self-Healing by Thought Force, YOGeBooks: Hollister, MO, pg.17;*

38. *William Walker Atkinson - The Secret of Mental Magic, A course of seven lessons, YOGeBooks: Hollister, MO, pg. 184, 53, 150;*

39. *Kybalion - Studiu asupra filozofiei ermetice a vechiului Egipt si a vechii Elade de trei inițiați, Editor Henri Durville, Paris, format PDF decsărcat de pe internet, pg. 51, 17, 13, 14, 58, 90, 17, 30, 20, 4;*

40. *Tăblițele de Smarald ale lui Thoth Atlantul, Editura Atma Mundi, București, 2014; pg. 39, 41, 98, 38, 40, 92, 39, 40, 81;*

41. *Legile lui Zamolxis;*

42. *https://quantumuniversity.com/quantum-medicine/morphogenetic-fields;*

43. *E-Motion - film documentar;*

44. *Manuela Timofte - Colecție personală de citate;*

45. *Manuela Timofte - Rețeta Fericirii - 5 ingrediente comune, Smashwords, 2023, Draft2Digital, 2024;*

46. *Manuela Timofte - Jurnal personal;*

❀✲☙❧✲❀

About the Author

Manuela was born in a small town in Transylvania, Romania, and grew up under the communist regime. Her childhood dream was to become a teacher, and this dream, once realized, kept her motivated for over 20 years.

She obtained her BA in English and then BA in Psychology at Spiru Haret University. After the age of 40, she earned an MA in developmental psychology from Oxford Brookes University.

She worked as a teacher in different schools in Hunedoara and Cluj-Napoca. After leaving the country, she worked in the UK for several years with children and adults with special needs. During her master's studies, she tutored Muslim children in Oxford. After completing her Masters, she was part of the IELTS exam administration team at Ealing Hammersmith and West London College. She also worked as a volunteer for one of the Marie Curie shops in the UK.

Upon returning to the country, she worked as a volunteer psychologist for autistic children within the Association "Autism-Lumea Mea" in Hunedoara, and for a short time, as a psychologist at DGASPC Hunedoara.

Currently, she is a volunteer editor for the Spanish platform Masticadores, writes books on spirituality, edits books, and offers support to those who want to learn more about clearing negative emotions. She spends the rest of her time working in the garden, among trees and flowers.

You can contact her through her blog https://inalove.world/.

Published books:

35 Inspirational Quotes - 2020

40 Mesaje Inspiraționale - 2021

40 Inspirational Quotes - 2021

Rețeta Fericirii: 5 Ingrediente comune - 2023

Happiness Recipe: 5 Common Ingredients - 2023

Grădina Iubirii - Bogăția din Noi - 2024